LOCKLEAZE

IAN HADDRELL

The
History
Press

Taken in 1963 from a front bedroom of No. 98 Landseer Avenue, the home of the Godfrey family. No. 98 is located on the corner of Landseer Avenue and Crome Road. It has been suggested that members of the Rogers family are carrying out repairs to the car with its bonnet raised. Despite the surprising number of vehicles in the vicinity, the young boys seem quite content playing in the street. This part of Landseer Avenue featured briefly in a scene from the 1964 film *Some People*, starring Kenneth More and Ray Brooks.

First published 2010

The History Press
The Mill, Brimscombe Port
Stroud, Gloucestershire, GL5 2QG
www.thehistorypress.co.uk

© Ian Haddrell, 2010

The right of Ian Haddrell to be identified as the Author
of this work has been asserted in accordance with the
Copyrights, Designs and Patents Act 1988.

ISBN 978 0 7524 5407 8

Typesetting and origination by The History Press
Printed in Great Britain

CONTENTS

ACKNOWLEDGEMENTS

I would like to thank the following for supplying photographs and information for this book: ABC Television, Stuart Armsby, Cliff and Carol Ashton (née Holland), Valerie Atkinson (née Rowe), Christopher Bailey, Cedric Barker, Robert Barnes, Neil Bartle, Sylvia Barton (née Cooper), Michael Batt, Lesley Beacham (née Freestone), Steven Bevan, Bristol Central Library, *Bristol Evening Post*, *Bristol Evening World*, Bristol Record Office, Alan and Susan Brown (née Dawe), Geoffrey Bruce, Duncan and Hazel Campbell (née Cooper), Lynda Chudleigh (née Hemmings), Senga Clark (née Watson), Allan and Pamela Cole (née Henson), David Connelly, Peter and Mary Dainton (née Robbins), Michael and Hazel Day (née Jarrett), Paul Didcott, Dings Crusaders RFC, Eileen Douglas (née Gardner), Geoffrey Endicott, Paul Gardner, Mike Geraghty, Gloucestershire Record Office, Tony Godfrey, Beryl Gough, Kelvin and Lorraine Grainger (née Dowling), Martin Gregory, Diane Haddrell (née Stone), Rachel Hill, Michael A. Houlden, Revd Leslie Jones, Wendy Jones (née Harding), André and Sue Kirby (née Cook), Wendy Kirby (née Griffiths), Joy Langley, Celia Lawday (née Slowley), Gill Lawry (née Langley), Ronald Lloyd, Stephen Lloyd, Lockleaze Primary School, Lockleaze Secondary School, Robert Lott, Andrew and Liz Malpas (née Jay), Revd Ernest Marvin, Beth Millar, Martin Mills, Josephine Naylor (née Conlin), Derek Nethercote, Mike Oakley, Patricia Palmer (née Cox), Margaret Parker (née Batt), Brenda Parrott (née Cooper), Philip Parrott, George Pegler, Joyce Plummer, Reg Porter, Jill Preston (née Saunders), Roger Pritchard, David Richardson, Robert Richardson, Cynthia Rowe, Lindra Rowles (née Shore), Robert Smith, Martyn Smyth, Stan and Ann Stokes (née Seward), Marilyn Stone (née Gray), Stephen 'Sammy' Stride, Carole Tamlyn (née Pegler), Michael Thorpe, Regan 'DJ' Toomer, Paul Townsend, Cynthia Travers (née Carless), Michael and Sandra Truman (née Brennan), Maddy Wall, Michael Wall, *Western Daily Press*, Christine Welch (née Gadsby), Carole White (née Hobbs), Brenda Williams (née Hanks), Brian Winter, Lynda Wood (née Jay) and Paul Wootten.

A special thank you to Patrick 'Nobby' Clark and David 'Wally' Woolford for their time and effort in providing countless names and information to accompany the photographs, and for the many hours of entertainment they have provided with their stories of life in Lockleaze.

Every effort has been made to identify copyright holders of illustrations from published materials, but I apologize to anyone overlooked in my search, or to photograph owners should their names be omitted from the above list.

A crowd gathers in Lockleaze Secondary School playing field sometime in the 1950s. The event is probably one of the annual fêtes organised by the Lockleaze Community Association. Mrs Edna Robbins, her daughter Mary, Rosemary Salmon, Mr MacDowell and Patricia Malpas have been identified in the gathering. The row of houses beyond the field are homes in Hogarth Walk.

INTRODUCTION

Following the publication of *Lockleaze Schools*, which predominantly featured pictures of school life, this second volume of old photographs of Lockleaze focuses for the most part on the people, places, organizations and events of the estate. Two important aspects of Lockleaze history are included in this book that were only touched on previously, both of which have had a significant impact on the local community, albeit in very different ways. Firstly, the production of the passion play *A Man Dies* had a considerable influence on a generation of young people from the Lockleaze area in the 1960s; the second, the move by Shaftesbury Crusade to Lockleaze shortly after the building of the estate, provided a facility that enabled the establishment of a number of groups and clubs, the most significant being the Boys' Brigade and the creation of a permanent home for Dings Crusaders Rugby Club, who still remain at the heart of the Lockleaze community.

The current home of Dings Crusaders RFC was originally purchased in 1949 by the Lockleaze Recreation Ground Charitable Trust, a charity set up by the Shaftesbury Crusade in an effort to establish their mission in what was then a new council housing estate. Redland Park Church established a Sunday school and Boys' Brigade Company (the 50th Shaftesbury Crusade), but the creation of a church never actually got off the ground because a minister could not be found to run it. The Lockleaze site also became the new home of Dings Crusaders RFC and from 1954 the club started to build a strong relationship with the new Lockleaze Secondary School and the community in general, with the school providing young players for the club. However, in the early 1990s the Shaftesbury Crusade's congregation in Bristol dwindled and the responsibility of their Lockleaze site passed to the rugby club with the appointment of new trustees – currently the rugby club president, vice-president and chairman of selectors.

A Man Dies, conceived by the Revd Ernest Marvin and Old Vic Theatre actor Ewan Hooper, was an attempt to show the relevance of the Gospel in the twentieth century as well as to put the Bible story into the words and thoughts of the day. Both men were, and still are, members of the Iona Community, an ecumenical Christian community committed to seeking new ways of living the Gospel in today's world, which has a long-standing commitment to working with young people with or without religious connections.

The play was originally planned to only have been performed in St James' church hall, but having won a much larger audience when it was aired by independent television, it attracted a great deal of unexpected publicity, becoming front page news in the national press. During its seven-year existence, much controversy surrounded *A Man Dies*, with considerable opposition from people in this country and overseas. Words like 'scandalous', 'disgusting', 'blasphemous', and 'the Devil's work' were used to describe it. However, there was also a great deal of support for the play and in the 1960s it was presented live, on a smaller scale, by various churches and youth clubs in over 200 places in Britain. When the Lord Chamberlain refused to grant a licence for a public stage performance in Bristol in 1966, a deputation visited the Lord Chamberlain to discuss his policy of refusing to licence the portrayal of Christ on stage. Those supporting the deputation were the Archbishops of Canterbury and York, the Cardinal Archbishop of Westminster, the Bishops of Bristol and London, Sir Alec Guinness, Dame Flora Robson, Dame Sybil Thorndike, John Neville, Arnold Wesker, and others.

A Man Dies gave a great number of youngsters the opportunity to engage in a common project which required them to exercise qualities of discipline, loyalty and hard work. They found they could use their undisputed talents to some purpose, and were caught up in a drama which was meaningful and relevant to them. They got a tremendous kick out of doing something together, and graduated from the state of being just another club to being a real community, bound together by a common experience. In 1960, who could have imagined that a group of teenagers from Lockleaze, telling a story in their own language, would have entered the world of television studios, appeared on the front pages of national newspapers, been photographed by professional photographers, visited Birmingham, Manchester and Winchester College, performed at the Colston Hall and made an appearance at the Royal Albert Hall.

An interesting insight into the formative years of Lockleaze is obtainable from a contemporary piece of writing, 'Five Years in Lockleaze', an extract from an article that appeared in the local community periodical *Lockleaze Broadsheet*, dated June 1955 and priced at *2d*:

Five years ago about two thirds of the houses had been built, but otherwise there was only St Mary's Hall and Romney Avenue Junior School. Since then building has never stopped. Accommodation has been provided for ministers, doctors and the Police. But the new building has consisted mostly of flats, and how much difficulty would have been avoided if they had been made soundproof. (For the sake of those who will live in them in years to come, is it too much to hope that something will be done to improve them?) We have seen the building of two more fine schools, Primary and Secondary, and everybody will be particularly interested to see the development of the comprehensive system in the latter. Visiting tradesmen had served the needs of many houses (and still do), but everyone was glad to see the building of the six shops and the 'Co-op', and with flats over them. The high standard of public building was maintained with the building of the Presbyterian Church (called St James after the former Church in the Horsefair), and of the Community Centre by voluntary labour over the whole five years. On the whole we can be thankful and proud in the way in which our buildings have grown.

While the buildings have grown so have the institutions. Five years ago the Community Association and the congregations of the two churches had been formed, and there were and still are also two other Sunday Schools – the Ebenezer and Shaftesbury. All these have grown and expanded, especially as more premises became available. At the same time there has been growing co-operation between these organisations, and these have led to various new institutions. First of these was the Toc H branch, made up of men who had got to know each other building the Community Centre, and others from the churches. The Joint Council originally consisted only of representatives from the main organisations, but local councillors, doctors, teachers, and social workers now also have a part in its thinking about the needs of the whole estate. Some of these have been met through the Lockleaze Youth Centre (in St Francis' Hall), the Toddlers' Club, and the Pensioner's Club.

This volume also contains photographs of a range of sporting teams associated with Lockleaze and recalls the numerous individuals who have demonstrated their sporting prowess on the playing fields of Dings, Purdown, Bonnington Walk and the Lockleaze schools.

For Diane, my Lockleaze girl.

1

EARLY DAYS

Looking from Horfield Common, near the Wellington Inn public house, towards Purdown. The photograph, taken in 1897 by F. Snary of Castle Street, Bristol, shows one of a series of potential development sites for the Bristol Boundaries Committee, who at the time were looking to extend Bristol's boundaries. Gloucester Road is in the foreground, the industrial chimneys of Bristol in the distance.

George Müller's orphanage buildings, seen from Purdown, dominate the ridge at Ashley Down. Known for generations as the Müller Homes, their German immigrant founder was insistent on the title 'The New Orphan House' as he did not want his name to be prominent. In 1845, Müller (1805-1898), from Kroppenstedt, a village near Halberstadt in Prussia, entered into a contract for the purchase of the seven acres of ground at £120 per acre for the accommodation, feeding, clothing and education of 300 destitute and orphan children. On 18 June 1849, the orphans transferred to the new building.

'A Country Lane, Purdown' with two boys returning home carrying wood for the winter fire. The lane is probably Sir John's Lane, which originally ran from Stapleton to Horfield providing a means of access to Purdown Farm. The boundary wall of Heath House is on the right with open fields to the left that will become Lockleaze in the 1940s.

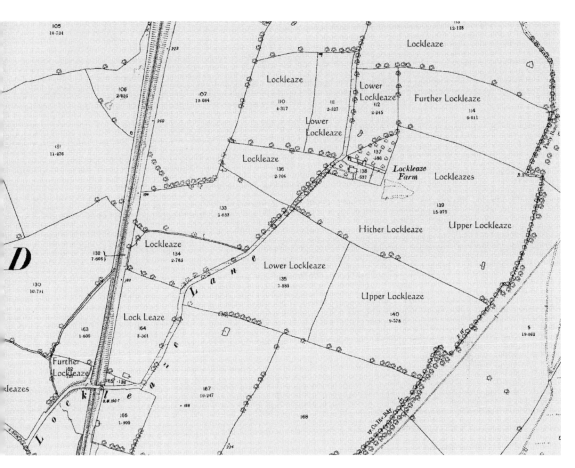

Lockleaze Farm, Lockleaze Lane and the main railway line are identifiable features on the 1881 Ordnance Survey map of part of Horfield parish. The farm, built between 1843 and 1851, was located at the top of Lockleaze Lane, which is clearly visible running from Berry Lane, across the railway line, to the farm buildings and beyond. Lockleaze Farm stood on the land between the terraced houses in Thornycroft Close and Nos 86 and 88 Bonnington Walk. James Saunders, born in Pensford, Somerset, began farming Lockleaze Farm from around 1880 until the 1920s, when a brother took over. James married Agnes Maria Hunt on 6 July 1887 at Horfield Parish Church, having five children between 1888 and 1897. The eldest son, Alexander, who farmed at Filton Hill Farm, bought a new Fordson tractor in the 1940s and won a contract with the John Laing building company hauling windows and joinery to their construction sites at Southmead, Lawrence Weston and Lockleaze.

Lockleaze School was built from 1951 to 1954 on the twelve-acre field, numbered 113, to the north of the farm. The relevant Lockleaze field names from the 1843 tithe map have been added. At their meeting on 12 July 1938, Bristol City councillors accepted the Housing Committee's proposal to buy, from Mrs R.G. Burden, an area of just over 112 acres between Purdown and the railway line for housing purposes.

Looking south from Bonnington Walk bridge towards Constable Road bridge. Opened on 14 May 1927 as Horfield Platform, the station's platforms and long footbridge are visible in the foreground. The station was rebuilt when the line was quadrupled through Horfield in the 1930s and its name was shortened to Horfield when it reopened on 30 April 1933. The station closed on 23 November 1964. The newly constructed Wordsworth Road is on the right.

Two photographs of Purdown Farm combined by Mike Houlden to give a composite image of the farmhouse and its outbuildings. The individual in front of the window is a member of the Gilbert family, the last occupants of the farm, who moved to Brangwyn Grove when the farm closed. During the nineteenth century the farm was occupied by various families, mostly farm labourers, although the 1881 census enumeration records Walter Champion, a dairyman employing two men, and his family living there. The farm, situated in a field known as Purdown or Stoney Furlong, was accessed by a track called Sir John's Lane.

Detail of a German aerial reconnaissance photograph taken by the Luftwaffe on Sunday 30 June 1940, ten days before the commencement of the Battle of Britain. Shaldon Road is the isolated row of houses off Muller Road in the bottom right of the picture. At the top end of Shaldon Road, at right angles, is the embryonic Lindsay Road. The Purdown anti-aircraft gun emplacements are visible (four gun-pits) at the end of Sir John's Lane. Eastville Stadium, home of Bristol Rovers Football Club, and the gasworks in Glenfrome Road, which has been marked as a potential target, are at the top of the picture.

In the build-up to the Second World War, the German air force realised that any successful invasion of Britain needed to be informed by up-to-date aerial intelligence, for pinpoint bombing of targets to disrupt the supply lines of the defending country. Swarms of specially adapted aircraft, flying as high as 37,000ft to avoid detection, photographed all the major cities, ports and military installations across a swathe of southern England, from Hampshire to the tip of Cornwall, carrying out the first ever aerial survey of the United Kingdom. The film was then taken back to their bases, developed and collated. The photographs were annotated with information as to the target subject, location, and the time that the picture was taken. Copies of the target photographs, together with maps, were then supplied to the bomber crews. The picture above is titled 'Stapleton Gas Works' and referenced TN1602.

Early stages of the construction of Lockleaze estate are evident from the road-building taking place in this 1946 aerial photograph. Brangwyn Grove, Constable Road, Cotman Walk, Landseer Avenue and Romney Avenue are in progress with, to the right of the line of trees, the outline of Gainsborough

Square. Lockleaze Farm is in the bottom right of the picture. The line of trees in the foreground marks the ancient parish boundary between Stapleton and Horfield. The two gasholders are in Dovercourt Road.

Workmen are still applying the finishing touches to Romney Avenue Junior School in 1949, even though the first pupils have already started the term. The infant and nursery schools to the north were constructed a year later. The open fields on the western flank of Purdown soon disappeared and were replaced by additional housing on Romney Avenue, and the houses of Gilray Close, Mulready Close and Rackham Close. The water tower in the distance supplied the camp on Purdown that supported the anti-aircraft gun site.

Lockleaze under construction, 1947. During the Second World War, Fred Pontin became involved with helping to establish hostels for construction workers and, using this experience, decided to venture into the holiday business by forming a company to buy an old disused camp at Brean Sands in 1946, where he opened the first Pontin's Holiday Camp. For a short period after the war ended, he remained in catering, running canteens for labourers who had been drafted in to build the Lockleaze housing estate.

2

PEOPLE AND PLACES

An early photograph of Romney Avenue, opposite Cameron Walk. The lady returning home with her shopping passes a variety of makes of motor vehicles parked outside St James' Church. Visiting tradesmen had served the needs of many houses prior to the building of the six shops and the Co-op on Gainsborough Square.

A Verrecchia's ice cream van parked at the top of Romney Avenue, *c*. 1961. The group of youngsters have just returned from a funfair held at the Memorial Ground, Filton Avenue. From left to right: David 'Ginger' Fugill, Cliff Ashton, John Kirby, Brian Henson, Jeanette Kirby, Paul Kirby. Brian Henson has won a couple of coconuts whilst Paul Kirby clutches a goldfish in a jam jar. To the right are the rear of the houses in Brangwyn Grove; the open grassland behind them became the site of the Pastime Centre.

Eugenio Verrecchia set up his ice cream business in Bristol in 1925 after emigrating from Italy to Britain around the turn of the century. He opened the city's first ice-cream parlour, the Modern Café in Coronation Road, Bedminster, where Italian-style ice cream was made in huge wooden vats. Eugenio started the business, but it was Romeo and Maria who made the Verrecchia name a byword for delicious ice cream in Bristol. Romeo was one of Eugenio's seven children, and he married Maria – known as Mrs V. to thousands of customers – in 1946. Romeo's brother Robert started a factory in Stockwood Road, Brislington, but it was Mrs V. who built up the fleet of vans which toured the city seven days a week. It was in 1960 that Verrecchia launched Bristol's first 'ice cream machine on wheels', as it was then called. It was a real novelty. A wide-eyed newspaper report stated:

It means, in effect, that ice cream is made only minutes before it is served, unlike the days, and perhaps weeks, which the family brick type of ice remains in the refrigerator. An additional motor is fitted to the van to supply the generating power which works the machine and runs the freezing apparatus. Each morning the vans will leave with a complete load of mixed ingredients and will not have to return to the depot for refills. Cones are filled with ice cream by a tap similar to a miniature bar pump. (Courtesy of Paul Townsend)

Taken on the central green of Haydon Gardens in 1962. From left to right: Martin Cox, Philip Barrett, Alan Mays and George Pegler. The boys, aged between sixteen and seventeen years and residents of Haydon Gardens, started at Lockleaze Secondary School in September 1957.

Carole Pegler, June Gilbert and Linda Hill pose in their finery – Linda in an orange skirt with white lines – outside the community centre in Gainsborough Square prior to going inside to a Wednesday night rock 'n' roll dance, 12 August 1959. Weekly dances were also held at St Francis' Church in Dovercourt Road and Bristol North Youth Club.

Barbara Harrison, Diane Stone and Melita Knowlson, photographed with Regan Toomer in the Dings playing field, Easter 1969, with the secondary school building in the distance. Diane, Melita and Regan started at Lockleaze in September 1966, with Barbara joining in January 1967 from Chorley Girls' School, Lancashire.

Cynthia Carless seated on the back of her boyfriend's scooter in the well-tended front garden of her home, No. 31 Bonnington Walk, in 1965. Cynthia met Nicky Hobbs on the No. 21 bus whilst travelling to the Corn Exchange in Bristol for the regular R&B nights. The teddy bear was a gift for Cynthia bought in Cornwall whilst Nicky was on holiday with a group of Mods. Apparently the bear was strapped to the front of the Vespa during the whole of the journey home!

A group of happy children gathered in the front garden of the Malpas home, No. 35 Constable Road, *c.* 1957. From left to right, back row: Carol Shortman, Patricia Malpas, Michael Walker and Eve Walker. Middle row: Timothy Barry, James Kilbane, Judith Barry and Christopher Lloyd. Front row: Andrew ?, -?-, Gregory Malpas and Mary Walker.

Cyril Rowe took over the chip shop on Gainsborough Square in 1951, at that time owned by Bristol City Council, continuing in business there until the mid-1960s. His wife, Ivy (née Comley), is stood outside the shop with Lilian Garland, the godmother of daughter Valerie Rowe, who was visiting from South Africa. In addition to selling fish and chips and wet fish, there was also a café providing hot and cold snacks, teas and beverages. The wet fish cabinet is visible in the shop window, with advertisements for fizzy drinks Tizer and Corona identifiable.

The Pastime Centre, Brangwyn Grove, built in the mid-1960s as a day centre for disabled people, shortly after its completion. During the great Bristol flood of July 1968, the building was one of a number of venues used by the Emergency Feeding Service and WRVS (Women's Royal Voluntary Service) as an emergency welfare centre, providing meals to homeless families.

The building was built around a square and this central section was an area where, on fine days, people who attended could sit outdoors. In the foreground is a well-stocked goldfish pond.

Julie Harris stood in Crome Road in 1964 beside a Mark One Scootacar belonging to her boyfriend, Tony Godfrey, with Thornycroft Close in the distance. The Scootacar was a British three-wheeled microcar built in Leeds by Scootacars Ltd, a division of the railway locomotive builder the Hunslet Engine Company between 1957 and 1964. It was allegedly built because the wife of one of the directors wanted something easier to park than her Jaguar. The shape of the car was designed by Henry Brown, who did it by sitting on a Villiers engine and then having an assistant draw an outline around him. The body was built in glass fibre and was very tall for its size, being 60in (1,524mm) high, 87in (2,210mm) long and only 52in (1,321mm) wide. It was nicknamed 'the telephone booth'. Two people could be carried with a passenger behind the driver or, alternatively, just squeezed in alongside. Power came from a Villiers 9E 197cc single cylinder two-stroke engine coupled to a four-speed motorcycle type gearbox and chain drive to the single rear wheel. Steering was by handlebars. The top speed was 50mph (80km/h).

Roger Pritchard, wearing his Lockleaze School blazer, with his cousin Trevor Towning, stood in front of the lake at Bristol Zoo in 1957. In one lapel is his Lonnie Donegan Fan Club badge and in the other a 50th (Shaftesbury Crusade) Company Boys' Brigade badge. Roger attained fame as Lee Sheriden, a member of the pop group the Brotherhood of Man. He co-wrote the 1976 Eurovision song contest winner 'Save Your Kisses For Me'.

Michael and Bernard Houlden with their cousin Clive Callaghan in around 1949, stood on the rough ground between Nos 4 and 5 Haydon Gardens before Purdown Farm was demolished to accommodate the building of Fairacre Close.

Mike Houlden recalls the demise of the farm:

The family who lived in the farm were called Gilbert and one name I remember was Cecil. I recall seeing cows in the big barn, which must have been around 1950, with two side-effects being the ripe smell and the plague of flies in our houses. There were always a few flying round and round the light in the living room, and every house used lots of rolls of sticky fly papers to trap them.

There was tall grass around the whole place, full of red flowers, grasshoppers and skylarks. There was also an old midden pile [refuse heap] next to the farm, well rotted, in which we kids used to dig for old bottles, the ones with glass balls built into the necks; we would smash the bottles to get these marbles out! In the tumble-down lean-to shed there was a farm cart stored, with its shafts held up with a small chain. As a small boy I once stood on this chain and bounced up and down between the shafts, until the chain snapped and my head slammed into the ground. It taught me a lesson!

The roof of the old barn, adjoining the shed, was of red tiles, some missing. As boys we would throw stones up to the roof and they would slide back down, sometimes dropping through the holes, a danger to those who dared venture into the barn. Near the lane was an old Anderson shelter left over from the Second World War, and we would set fires in it and then run in and out of the smoke wearing Dad's old gas mask.

The farm was abandoned about 1955, and we kids took some of the lead from the roof and melted it down to make blocks to load into our Dinky toy lorries to play with. When the buildings were finally pulled down shortly afterwards, thousands of house mice were made homeless, and moved into Haydon Gardens. We could hear them running about inside ceilings, and we all got cats to evict them, by pushing the cats under the floorboards in the bedrooms.

A well-known sight in the garden of No. 3 Haydon Gardens for over ten years was the 35ft boat built by George Pegler senior and his son, George junior. The hull was originally part of a lifeboat and the Peglers added a diesel engine and built the cabin, prior to transporting the vessel by trailer to Bristol docks, where it was moored for a number of years, making journeys up the River Avon to Keynsham and Bath.

The Co-operative Society's shop in Gainsborough Square nearing completion in August 1952. The Co-op multi-purpose store occupied all the commercial space on the north-eastern side of the square. At the same time, Bristol Corporation built six shops on the north-western side. An advertisement for the Co-op that appeared in an early issue of the local monthly magazine *Lockleaze Broadsheet*, published by the Anglican and Presbyterian churches in Lockleaze, informed residents that the store, in addition to the self-service grocery and a well-equipped food hall, contained butchery, drapery, footwear, furnishing and hardware departments.

Bernard Houlden sat astride his 350cc Triumph 21 motorcycle, Haydon Gardens, *c.* 1962. It cost £65, quite expensive for the time, and Bernie re-sprayed the bike to its original colour using his mum's vacuum cleaner – which 'turned out very well'. The seat was re-covered in blue with the side panels painted white. He also fitted Siamese exhaust pipes. 'The bike was looking so good I became concerned about driving it in case of an accident; so I sold it.'

At 11.30 a.m. on 10 March 1966, the Lord Mayor of Bristol and the Lady Mayoress (Alderman Thomas H. Martin, MBE, JP and Mrs Martin) were met by Councillor J. O'Neil (Chairman of Bristol Housing Committee) in Unity Chapel, Shaldon Road. They were visiting Lockleaze to inaugurate the Lockleaze Tree Belt and for the Lady Mayoress to cut a ribbon across the entrance to Danby House to mark the completion of 642 new homes in Bristol. Danby House, the block of flats in the centre of the picture, together with Morris Road and Downman Road, were part of the provision of 251 homes on three adjoining sites in Lockleaze.

'The Leaze', No. 23 Romney Avenue, was officially opened on Thursday 14 February 1963 by the Lord Mayor of Bristol, Alderman L.K. Stevenson. The house, one of a number of family-group homes specially designed by the City Architect, consisted of a 'family' of ten children, ages ranging from four to thirteen years, and the house-parents. The aim of the family-group home was that 'the ten children should grow up in an atmosphere and environment as near as possible to that which would be enjoyed by any ordinary natural family.'

Sylvia Jackson, the lady on the left, who was assistant house-mother at the time, stood outside of the 'The Leaze' with a group of children, *c.* 1963. It was here that she first met her future husband, the Revd Leslie Jones, when he gave the dedication and blessing at the official opening of the home in February 1963. 'The Leaze' finally closed in 2004.

A group of children from Haydon Gardens congregate, around 1950, in and around George Pegler's 1937 Morris 8 motor car that he rebuilt, having found it abandoned in Romney Avenue. George, who with his brothers ran a business in Horfield manufacturing touring caravans, took the finished car on camping holidays to Nice, Paris, Germany, Austria and Switzerland, securing their luggage to the sides of the vehicle. From left to right, pictured behind the car: George Pegler junior, -?-, David Johnson, Bernard Houlden, Alan Mays and Philip Barrett. Seated in the car: -?-, Kathleen Wilson, Carole Pegler, Eileen Smith and Patricia Cox. Stephen Bull is stood with his black Labrador, Rex.

A No. 2 bus service to Lockleaze, parked at the Sea Mills terminus, *c.* 1952. This was the second service, after the No. 21 route, extended to serve Lockleaze in 1948. The initial route of the No. 2 went along Brangwyn Grove to Gainsborough Square as, when it was introduced, there were no houses at the top end of Romney Avenue. A number of bus drivers and conductors were residents of Lockleaze operating out of the Muller Road garage.

A Bedford coach owned by Mr Jacobs of No. 39 Cotman Walk parked outside his home in October 1964. Herbert Jacobs purchased the vehicle in 1963 from Jimmy Miller, a bus and coach operator and vehicle dealer, using the coach as a mobile grocer and greengrocer's shop. Another local resident, Mr John Shorland of Brangwyn Grove, ran a thirty-one seater Commer coach, LHU 211, from December 1954 to December 1957.

Edward Houlden and son Bernard stood in Haydon Gardens in 1962 beside a Bedford van belonging to Eddie's employer, Mr Freeman, who allowed Eddie to take it home for private use and commuting to work. It had sliding doors, a split windscreen and a propensity for the front wheels to fall off! The vertical bar, just visible on the van's front wing, is the old-style trafficator indicator that used to pop out to indicate turning. Presumably the covering over the bonnet and radiator grill is to aid winter starting!

GUN LICENCE (10s.)   EW   004888
(NOT TRANSFERABLE)

MR   MICHAEL   ANTHONY   HOULDEN

(Full Christian names and Surname in block letters)

of   H,   HAYDON   GARDENS   LOCKLEAZE

(Full postal address)   (See Note 1 below)

BRISTOL 7

is hereby licensed, subject to the requirements of the law, to CARRY AND USE A GUN in Great Britain and Northern Ireland from the date hereof until and including the **31st JULY** next following.

Issued at   2   hours   25   minutes   p. m. o'clock
at the place and on the date indicated by the Issuing Office

stamp, by   B Cooper

Issuing Office Stamp — LOCKLEAZE BRISTOL 27 AU 66

WARNINGS
1. This licence does not authorise any person to purchase, have in his possession, use or carry any firearm (as defined in the Firearms Act, 1937) in respect of which it is necessary to hold a firearm certificate granted under the said Act unless he holds such certificate, nor any air weapon or shot gun except as permitted by the Air Guns and Shot Guns, etc., Act, 1962.
2. Certain game and wildfowl may not be killed during close seasons or are entirely protected. A sportsman should ascertain the effect of the law before he goes shooting.
3. The land-owner's permission to shoot must be obtained.

NOTES
1. Any permanent change of address should be notified to the County or County Borough Council in whose area the Licensee's former address is situate.
2. Attention is drawn to the suggestions for ensuring clean kills on the back of this licence.

The gun licence issued to Michael Houlden on 27 August 1966 at Lockleaze Police Station. Before 1966, shotguns were on open sale to anyone and could be carried around without a problem. The shotgun licence was introduced after Harry Roberts shot and killed two London police officers with an illegal handgun in August 1966. The Firearms Act required, for the first time, that persons had to obtain a licence before acquiring a shotgun.

Shaftesbury Crusade huts, Landseer Avenue, 1952. Following the development of Lockleaze, a field was acquired by Shaftesbury Crusade and new huts were erected with changing rooms for sport and a plunge bath. This was opened by the Lord Mayor of Bristol, Alderman F.A. Steadman, JP, the opening ceremony being followed by a rugby match between veterans and present members, and a Boys' Brigade football match. The venue was used by the Boys' Brigade, Life Boys, Girls Life Brigade (Captain Mrs Doreen Oliver) and for a youth club run by Mrs Boaler. As Lockleaze was a new estate with a high population, a Sunday school was started, with 100-plus scholars, under the leadership of Mr Jack Harris.

A hand-drawn Christmas card dated 1969. Drawn by Keith Elsbury of No. 14 Haydon Gardens, a talented commercial artist, it depicts Keith in his MG sports car, which he occasionally raced around the Castle Combe motor racing circuit. The passenger is his then girlfriend, Geraldine Yates. Keith attended art school after leaving Lockleaze School in 1957.

Mrs Violet Shore, holding her youngest child, Ian, stood in the front garden of her home, No. 107 Landseer Avenue, June 1948. Her daughter, Lindra, recalls the family's early days in Lockleaze:

We moved into 107 Landseer Avenue late in 1947. I can remember my sister Denise and I travelling in the back of the removal van with Dad while Mum came on the bus with Ian who was a babe in arms. He was born at the end of September 1947, so was probably only two to three months old if that. Mum is now ninety-three and can't remember the exact month we moved in but it was probably October or November. I was nearing my fourth birthday and Denise was just two years old. I remember there seemed to be a lot of mud and just pavements and garden paths, no gardens as they were fenced off. Then other families started to arrive, but only on our side as the houses on the other side of the road were still being built, and I recall that a lorry or van would turn up during the day and someone would call 'tea up' and the builders would come out with their jerry cans to be filled with hot tea. I played on the site one Sunday when I had been told to stay away and ruined my best pair of red patent leather shoes. Did I get into trouble! Eventually, the other houses were built, occupied, and friendships were made that lasted a life time. The children grew up, married and moved away, but for some of us, that friendship has carried on and we are still in touch. Looking back, we realize what a wonderful playground we had and how lucky we were being able to play in fields, making dens out of old bits of corrugated tin, building camp fires and swinging from the trees with old lengths of rope. There were three trees growing on the green in Crome Road, one of which had divided itself and was known to all us children as the 'split tree'. We could roam over the Duchess estate and wander down to Snuff Mills, play in the farmers' fields, and be gone all day with a bag of jam sandwiches and a bottle of water, and be quite safe. Happy days!

Three friends resplendent in their new school uniforms as they prepare to set off for their first day at Lockleaze Secondary School in September 1959. From left to right: Cynthia Carless, Nina Brain and Loraine Trusler.

The construction of St James' Church on Romney Avenue is well underway in this photograph, *c.* 1952. It was built by the Presbyterian Church to replace the old St James' Church in the Horsefair, Bristol, which had been destroyed in 1940 during the Blitz. The congregation united with Trinity Presbyterian Church, Cranbrook Road, and the church was opened to serve all church people in Lockleaze. The foundation stone of the new church was laid by Dr Joseph Bacon, Moderator of the General Assembly, 17 November 1951. The cost of the stained-glass window was £850, the theme of which is 'The Coming of the Holy Ghost', and took fourteen months to complete.

The rear of the church looking towards Romney Avenue, showing the completed hall at the rear of the building. A larger hall was added later which was used for many community activities, including a youth club and rehearsals of the passion play *A Man Dies*. The hall was sold to Lockleaze Community Association in the 1980s.

Revd Michael Whitehorn, the first minister of St James', Lockleaze, with church members gathered outside the newly constructed building. Michael Drummond Whitehorn (1922-1999), the son of Revd Roy Whitehorn, one time principal of Westminster College, Cambridge, and Constance Ryley served at Lockleaze from 1951 to 1955. He left Bristol to take up a position in Lewisham, being replaced at Lockleaze by the Revd Ernest Marvin.

One of Revd Martin's initiatives was to open St James' Youth Club on Sunday evenings following the forty-five minute church service; the only proviso being that youngsters attended the evening service if they wanted to use the club. From left to right, front row: Marion Hawker, Linda Hewitt and Susan Bailey. The girl sat two rows back on the left is thought to be Wendy Skidmore.

St Mary's Church confirmation group photographed in the garden of The Parsonage, Copley Gardens, 1960. From left to right, back row: -?-, Stephen Hall, -?-, -?-. Third row: Rachel Adams, Owen Morey, -?-, -?-, Patricia Malpas, Lynda Jay, -?-, Gillian Gomm, Clive Dibbins, Mary Shaddick, Aubrey Newport, Susan Brooks, Revd Ralph Scrine, Mrs Joan Scrine. Second row: Lorraine Gibbard, Veronica Keefe, -?-, Sister Caunt. Front row: Revd David Skinner, Barbara Hale, Sandra Sheppard, Linda Bush.

St Mary's Church choir in the 1950s, a period when choir practice was held on Friday evenings at 7.00 p.m. From left to right, back row: unknown. Third row: -?-, Frank Payne, -?-, Mr Percival 'Pat' O'Keefe, -?-, -?-, Roger Jacobs. Second row: Allan Emery, Christopher Parrott, Duncan Campbell, David Critchley, -?-, -?-, -?-, Peter Gibbs, -?-. Front row: Clive Dibbins, Stephen Parrott, -?-, Revd Eric Huband, Revd Ralph Scrine, Mr A.E. Jeffery (churchwarden), Terry Gould, -?-, Alan Lamb.

3

EVENTS

A group of children in their Sunday best clothes, enjoying a summer occasion, possibly a garden fête, in the grounds of St James' Church sometime in the late 1950s. The boy standing appears to be conducting with two candyfloss. Judging by the drums on the grass, a band is in attendance.

1956

President :	Mr. C. V. DIBB
Vice-Presidents:	Mrs. J. WILKINS
	Mr. R. MUNDAY

OFFICERS

Chairman :	Mr. J. B. WATSON
	20 Brangwyn Grove
Vice-Chairman :	Mr. S. E. PRATT
	91 Brangwyn Grove
Hon. Secretary :	Mrs. J. WILKINS
	50 Landseer Avenue
Asst. Hon. Secretary :	Mr. S. E. PRATT
	91 Brangwyn Grove
Hon. Treasurer :	Mr. J. C. WATSON
	20 Brangwyn Grove
Asst. Hon. Treasurer:	Mrs. D. PERRY
	41 Hogarth Walk

Any questions regarding Membership to be addressed to the Chairman as membership Secretary.

Regular Social Events are held at the Community Centre. Details of these well attended functions are published regularly in the "Community News" and the local Press.

Above: The official opening of Lockleaze Community Centre, Gainsborough Square, took place on Saturday 2 April 1955. The opening ceremony was performed by MacDonald Hobley, one of the main BBC television announcers from 1946 to 1956, pictured second from the left in the front row. He was the first host of *Come Dancing* and was voted Television Personality of the Year 1954. The lady to his right is Mrs Lilian Watson, wife of the Community Association's first chairman. John Watson is the man wearing spectacles towards the rear, with his son Clifford (the Honorary Treasurer) looking over his shoulder. The three girls from left to right in the front row are Senga Watson, Judith Lovemore and Diane Perry. Mrs Eileen Lovemore and her son, Derek, have also been identified in the photograph. During the opening ceremony, Senga Watson presented a bouquet of flowers to Mrs Hobley

Left: The executive committee of Lockleaze Community Association, taken from a 1956 membership book. One of the aims of the association was 'to promote the well-being of the Community resident in the area known as Lockleaze Housing Estate, by means of encouraging and providing facilities for educational, social and moral development...'.

Lockleaze Community Association organised two annual events for the community and local residents gather in Hogarth Walk on the occasion of a summer fête held in the fields at the top of Landseer Avenue, *c.* 1952. The children on the horse-drawn cart are in fancy dress. Stood on the cart are: Senga Watson, fourth from the left, John Doling to her left, with his sister Valerie next to him. Colin Yeo, dressed as a jockey is at the very back, and Rita Yeo is second from the right. Brothers David and George Hunt are the small boys stood next to each other on the pavement at the front, holding the Bisto advertisement.

The opening of the summer fête, August Bank Holiday 1951, included an appearance by the 'Good Quads'. Daughters of Charles and Margaret Good of Westerleigh, Bridget, Frances, Elizabeth and Jennifer were born in June 1948, arousing great interest as they were the first quadruplets in the world to survive a caesarean section birth. The girls, with white ribbons in their hair, are pictured taking part in a tricycle race, won by one of the quads.

Above: Lockleaze won an inter-secondary schools 'It's a Knockout' competition in the mid-1990s. The event took place on Durdham Down, Bristol, and involved different types of obstacle courses that each member of the team had to negotiate. The event ended in a draw, the decider being a tug-of-war contest, which Lockleaze won. From left to right, standing: Jairzinho Wright, Danny Stevens, Andrew Balasco, Richard Sumner, Louisa Clarke, Donna Parsons. Kneeling: Jason Kinman, Emma Beasmore, Andrew Thomas, Rebecca Webley, Simon Smith. Paul Roberts, PE teacher and coach of the successful team, is in front.

Left: Prince Philip during his visit on 30 October 1959 to Lockleaze School's 'Wheatsheaf Club', the after-hours organisation run by Mr W.T. Baker promoting the Duke of Edinburgh's Award Scheme. At a draughts game, he paused and asked one of the players, Richard Newton, 'You've got him stuck, haven't you?' He looked amusedly at the boy's opponent, fifteen-year-old Paul Gardner, and added, 'Jolly good!' From left to right: Richard Newton, Prince Philip, headmaster Dr W.N. Littlejohns, Terry Parkinson, Paul Gardner.

Some of the group of Landseer Avenue neighbours who travelled to Weymouth on Saturday 16 August 1952. The street outing was organised by Mr Reg Harding, who at the time was employed as a coach driver. It was considered a wonderful treat as none of the families had cars and it was probably the first time any of the children had been farther than Weston-super-Mare. Stood at the rear is Mr Albert Shore. From left to right, seated in deck-chairs: Mrs Violet Shore, Mrs Iris Adams, Mrs Hilda Godfrey, Mrs Phyllis Phillips, Mr Albert Phillips. In front: Mr Alfred Godfrey, Maureen Phillips.

'Johnnie', played by Ray Brooks, rides his motorbike up Landseer Avenue towards Bonnington Walk, with Crome Road on the right, in a scene from the 1962 film *Some People*. The film starred Kenneth More, Ray Brooks, David Hemmings, David Andrews, Angela Douglas, Harry H. Corbett, Richard Davis, Frankie Dymon, Michael Gwynn and Anneke Wills. Many of the scenes were shot in and around Lockleaze, with the interior shots of Johnnie's home filmed in No. 95 Landseer Avenue.

Left: Carole Pegler of Haydon Gardens was prominent in the local beauty contest scene during the early 1960s. One of the highlights of her beauty queen career was when she was placed first in a regional heat of the Miss England contest held at the Locarno Ballroom, The Glen, Bristol, in 1961. At the time, eighteen-year-old Carole was a police cadet with Bristol Constabulary. Other local successes included: first place in the Milk for Beauty Swimsuit contest in 1961, and third in the Miss UK Area Finals, behind Maureen Gay and Marilyn Samuel. These events also took place at The Glen ballroom, near Durdham Down. Carole is pictured on the seven-platform diving board in Weston-super-Mare's open-air swimming pool during the Miss Weston-super-Mare beauty contest on a sunny summer day in 1962.

Below: This group of contestants in the *Bristol Evening Post* Holiday Princess beauty contest 1962-1963 includes Celia Slowley (No. 7) and Carole Pegler (No. 11). Celia, another local beauty from Horfield, was also a pupil at Lockleaze School.

Left: For being placed first in the regional heat of the Miss England beauty contest in 1961, Carole was presented with a cheque for £10 and a free trip to Newcastle-upon-Tyne in March to compete in the finals.

Below: The service for the opening and dedication of Lockleaze Church (St James'), conducted by the Moderator of the General Assembly (of the Presbyterian Church) The Right Reverend Andrew Prentice, took place on Wednesday 29 October 1952. From left to right: Revd Peter McCall (minister of Trinity Presbyterian Church, Cranbrook Road), Revd Michael D. Whitehorn (minister of St James' Church), Right Revd Andrew Prentice.

Paul Gardner, pictured in a posed *Bristol Evening Post* photograph, pointing at the tree on Gainsborough Square that was struck by a bolt of lightning. During the storm in 1955, local houses were also struck by lightning, resulting in many tiles being damaged and dislodged from roofs.

Mary Robbins, Georgina Forse and Carole Hobbs make the acquaintance of a member of the Household Cavalry and his mount at Horse Guards Parade during a Lockleaze School visit to London in the summer of 1958. The group also visited the Tower of London and Tower Bridge.

The Revd Leslie J. Jones married Sylvia M. Jackson on 17 October 1964 at St Mary's Church, Gainsborough Square. The Revd Jones served as vicar of St Mary Magdalene with St Francis for ten years from 1962. Members of the local Brownie pack form the guard of honour, which includes Julie Naish, Elizabeth Jay and Diane Stone.

A children's Christmas party in St Mary's church hall, 1954, attended mostly by residents of Romney Avenue. From left to right, standing adults: Mrs Gladys Batt, Mrs Kathleen Gray, 'Grandmother' Feveyear, -?-, Mrs Beryl Butcher, Mrs Clara Willis, -?-, Mrs Florence Feveyear, Audrey Smythe, Mrs Zena Williams, Mrs Joyce Donadel, Mrs Ivy Dawe, Mrs Joan Conlin, Mrs Mollie Moore, Mrs Winifred Bamford. Children standing behind far table: Lesley Gardner, Eileen Gardner, Patricia Olive, Yvonne Olive, Rita Donadel, Jeffrey Donadel, Raymond Dawe, Susan Dawe, Susan Moore, Paul Moore, Vincent Moore, Austin Bamford. Seated at far table: Paul Gardner, Alan Gardner, Kathleen Feveyear, Valerie Bundy, -?-, Keith Willis, -?-, -?-, Barry Conlin, David Jordan, David Conlin, -?-. Seated at near table facing the camera: -?-, Dorothy Smythe, John Smythe, Albert Bundy, Anthony Gray, Desmond Tippins, Billy Williams, Philip Williams, Richard Newton. Seated nearest camera: Ann Batt, Michael Batt, John Batt, Margaret Batt, Wendy Butcher, Christopher Butcher. Eileen Gardner, who lived in Romney Avenue, remembers the occasion well, despite her young age, 'Probably because it was such a splendid party, with games, delicious party food and gifts for all the children'.

The focal point of the photograph is a premature baby nearing her first birthday – unusual in those days as tiny babies rarely survived. Her name is Sandra Olive (born 6 January 1953), the daughter of Reginald and Joyce Olive who lived in Romney Avenue. From left to right, looking on, are: her sisters Patricia, aged eight, and Yvonne, Audrey Smythe, Lesley Gardner, Paul Gardner, Malcolm Gray. The little girl peeping round the baby, who appears to be enjoying cream cakes, is Eileen Gardner. Mrs Ivy Dawe and Mrs Joyce Donadel are the ladies looking on.

Children gather in fancy dress costumes for a coronation party for Queen Elizabeth II, June 1953, in front of Nos 190 and 192 Romney Avenue, homes of the Drew and Woodland families respectively. From left to right, back row: John Smythe, ? Butcher, Ann Batt, Marlene Jefferies, Yvonne Olive, Patricia Olive, Jean Smythe, Raymond Dawe, Dorothy Smythe, Keith Willis, Barry Conlin. Front row: ? Smythe, -?-, Colin Smythe, Vincent Moore, Kathleen Feveyear, Margaret Batt, Susan Dawe, Edwin Willis, Rosemary Lifton.

Another street party to celebrate the Queen's coronation in 1953. This one took place on the central green of Haydon Gardens. From left to right, back row: -?-, Jean Whittle, Valerie Sweet (?), Irene Collings, Carole Pegler. Front row: Martin Cox, Penelope Barrett, Patricia Cox, Gordon Johnstone, May Johnstone. All children attending school were given a souvenir coronation mug.

An additional party for the Queen's coronation took place at the end of Landseer Avenue at what is now Dings Crusaders Rugby Club. Entrants for the Dings fancy dress competition included, from left to right: Christopher, Philip and Stephen Parrott, who lived in Landseer Avenue. Chris is dressed as Arthur English (his usual persona was a stereotypical wartime 'spiv'), Phil as a Hula girl and Steve as Old Mother Riley. Old Mother Riley was a music hall act which ran from about 1934 to 1954, the part of the Irish washerwoman played by Arthur Lucan.

Landseer Avenue coronation street party. The street's men folk line up for the start of the Dads' race, the joint between the concrete road sections used as the starting line. From left to right: -?-, Mr Robert Donachie, Mr Albert Phillips, Mr Reginald Radnedge, Mr Alfred Godfrey, Mr Reginald Harding, -?-. Ian Shore is the young lad in guardsman fancy dress.

Ian, Lindra and Denise Shore pose outside of their home, decorated for the occasion, in fancy dress costumes during the Landseer Avenue coronation street party. The fancy dress competition, won by Denise, was judged by Mrs Beatrice Burgess, the proprietor of the Post Office in Gainsborough Square.

A special service was held at St Mary's Church in 2000 to celebrate the millennium, to which past church members and clergy were invited. Photographed in front of the altar in the refurbished church are, from left to right: Bishop Ian Brackley (curate to Revd Thompson-Glover), Canon Paul Dennyer (1988-1997), Canon Hugh Thompson-Glover (1972-1976), Revd Karen MacKinnon (1998-2000), Revd Leslie Jones (1962-1972), Revd Ralph Scrine (1952-1962), Bishop Roy Screech. Clive Royden Screech lived in Romney Avenue and attended St Mary's Youth Club. He is currently Bishop of St Germans in Cornwall. The Right Revd Ian Brackley is the Suffragan Bishop of Dorking.

Brian Winter receives applause from members of Dings Crusaders Rugby Club on the occasion of his 1,000th appearance for the club on Sunday 21 January 2001. Brian began his rugby career with Dings Crusaders in 1962, completing 1,121 games for the club before his retirement from the game in 2005. To mark the auspicious event, a team of former Bristol players played a Dings Crusaders XV at their Lockleaze home, the ex-Bristol XV winning the match by 'quite a lot to not very many' recalled Brian. The score was actually 60-20.

4

SPORT AND RECREATION

Lockleaze Rovers football team, photographed at Lockleaze playing fields, Purdown, around 1948, was formed by the first residents of Lockleaze, mostly ex-servicemen. From left to right, back row: -?-, -?-, -?-, Ronald Lloyd, Bert Jacobs, Charlie Sheppard, -?-, Reginald Bundy, William Brown (committee member), William Pritchard. Front row: Wilfred Barrett, Harry Rylatt, 'Rusty' Jacobs (mascot), George Bull, Reginald Bull, William Russ. Bill Pritchard, the referee, was also a local resident.

Lockleaze United Football Club had a successful period in the early 1970s with this group of players. From left to right, back row: Peter Millard (manager), Clive Budding, Martin Sedlan, John Hicks, Jamie Pegler, Andrew Priest, Mark Caines. Front row: David Williams, Martin Mills, Timmy Bryson, Steve Buckland, Colin Pitt, Philip Gibbs, Gary Britton, Dennis Southard. Honours included: 1971/72 (Under-13) Bristol Junior League winners; 1972/73 (Under-14) GYFA (Wilfred Osbourne) Cup winners, beating Lydney Town 2-0 in the final at Eastville Stadium; Bristol Junior League Cup winners; Bristol Junior League runners-up and 1973/74 (Under-15) Bristol Junior League winners.

Shaftesbury Crusade Football Club, 1982/83. From left to right, back row: Alex Bostrom (joint-manager), Ian Findlay, Stephen Wheeler, Paul Winter, Gary Merrick, Adrian Harvey, Colin Peters, Clive Graham, Alan Walsh (joint-manager). Front row: Michael Hannam, Jimmy Nutt, Colin Clark, Martin Mills, Keith Woodland, Terry Mahoney. The team were County of Avon Premier Combination Division One runners-up the season this picture was taken. Shaftesbury Crusade started in the Bristol Church of England League in the 1950s, when late president Wilf Barrett and Reg Bull ran the club. The team joined the Bristol District League in the early 1960s.

Many boys who attended Lockeaze School joined Manor Farm Boys' Club in the 1960s and 1970s, particularly to play in the football teams organised by the Horfield club. This is the Under-15 team of the 1969/70 season, taken on Horfield Common. From left to right, back row: Mr John Walters (manager), Roger Harper, Neil Greatorex, Keith Smith, Jeffrey Hancock, Philip Cross, Glen Marshall. Front row: Steven Barry, Ian Haddrell, Anthony Hiscox (captain), Stephen Barker, David Champion. All except Champion attended Lockleaze. Martin English, John Fisher, Mark Leonard, Christopher McGrane, Clive Hiscox and Frank Morse were other Lockleaze pupils who played for the team during that season.

The start of the senior event in the Bristol Battalion Boys' Brigade annual cross-country races, held at Ashton Court, Bristol. Five competitors from the 50th Company are on the right of the picture, in dark vests, from left to right: Keith Jarrett, Dennis Sanigar, Brian Winter, Patrick Clark, Peter Frampton. Patrick Clark was second in the race, Dennis Sanigar third, behind winner Lewis Lintern of the 38th Company, centre of the picture.

Members of 'Paddy' Webb's ballet class during a rehearsal for a show, *c.* 1955. Miss Webb ran dance classes from the late 1940s, when Lockleaze was built, to the 1960s, providing instruction in ballet, tap and modern dance. The classes were attended mostly by girls, although some boys did join the tap lessons. Examinations took place at Miss Love's studio in Ashley Down Road. From left to right, back row: Margaret Green, Yvonne Olive. Middle row: Lindra Shore, Patricia Olive, Valerie Bray. Front row: Christine Gadsby, Rita Sheppard, Ann Lyons, Sally Donachie, Marilyn Gray, -?-, Lesley Freestone.

Saturday morning classes for the youngest members were held in the community centre hut on Gainsborough Square, with twice-weekly classes held in St Mary's church hall. The group also performed in shows at the Colston Hall. From left to right, standing: Valerie Doling, -?-, -?-, -?-, -?-, -?-, -?-, Clare ?. Sitting: Lesley Freestone, Rosemary Lamb, Christine Gadsby. The unidentified dancers in the back row were members of Paddy Webb's Fishponds dance class.

Filton Avenue Junior Mixed School football team, who played in blue shirts, 1965. From left to right, back row: Mr Chivers (headmaster), Kevin Haddrell, John Mills, John Bennett, Stephen Dan, Robert Fionda, Mr Lawson. Middle row: Colin Boulton, George Bayliss, Steven Barry, Philip Cross, Martin Jefferies. Front row: Jamie Fudgell, Anthony Hiscox. All the boys, except for Haddrell, the author's cousin, and Mills, attended Lockleaze Secondary School, commencing in September 1966.

A group of fourth-year girls in Lockleaze School's playing field, taking a break during a school tennis lesson, 19 June 1959. From left to right, back row: Maureen Haskins, Linda Hill, Janet Conibear, Lindra Shore. Front row: Christine Ward, June Gillard, Jeannette Bush, Diane Smale.

Lockleaze School First XV rugby team, 1974. From left to right, back row: -?-, Gerald Rich, Kevin Brain, David Wheeler, Christopher Mills, Jeffrey Wiltshire. Middle row: David Williams, Robert Bryant, Neil Mattock, Martin Mills, Terry Bryant. Front row: Edmund Reid, Steven Appleford, Gary Britton, Dion Limb.

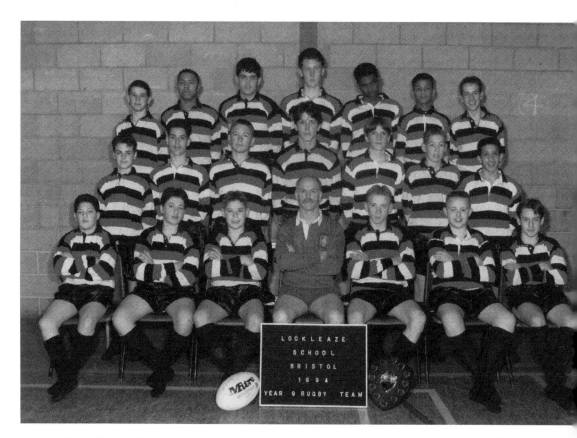

Lockleaze School Year 9 rugby team, 1994. From left to right, back row: Mark Uzzell, Darren Giddings, Simon Smith, Richard Sumner, Christopher Howard, Lloyd Thomas, Andrew Thomas. Middle row: Mark Searle, Andrew Balasco, Wayne Jones, Kevin Peacock, Alex Murray, Darren Walmsley, Jairzinho Wright. Front row: Wayne Fearon, Craig Moore, Tom Jenkins, Mr Paul Roberts (PE teacher), Danny Stevens, Gary Williams, Jason Kinman.

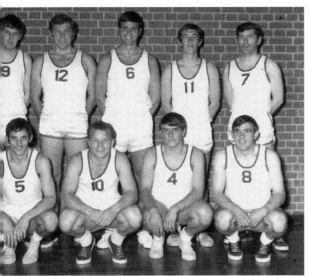

The Wheatsheaf basketball team, assembled in Lockleaze School gymnasium, *c.* 1968. From left to right, back row: Trevor Denley, Richard Hook, Lawrence Lloyd, Mark Buchaly, Robert Beynon. Front row: Martin Carter, Patrick Clark, Anthony Edwards, Stephen Bull. The Wheatsheaf team, run by PE teacher Terry Allen, was an 'out of school' team made up of lads who had attended Lockleaze School. The school youth club was called the 'Wheatsheaf Club' and was held on two evenings a week, so the sporting arm of that club was known as the Wheatsheaf. The team enjoyed excellent success in the West of England basketball league for a number of years before eventually disbanding.

Wheatsheaf basketball B-team. From left to right, back row: John Phillips, Brian Edmonds, David Isaac. Front row: Stephen Hook, Mark ?, Mark Buchaly, Alan Searle.

EARLY HISTORY OF DINGS CRUSADERS RFC

The 'Dings' was a notorious area of poverty and deprivation in the St Philips area of Bristol, between Temple Meads and Barton Hill. The Revd Uriah Thomas (1839-1901), minister of Redland Park Church from 1862 to 1901, was aware of the dreadful conditions in the Dings area, where a coffee house and meeting place called Shaftesbury Hall had been opened by the Bristol City Mission in an attempt to draw men away from the many local public houses. Hitherto, they were the only places where they could find some social life and escape from the crowded, dingy, insanitary houses, but where they spent their few shillings of pay, leaving practically nothing for their struggling wives to feed and bring up families. The Revd Thomas devised a scheme which had a double benefit. He knew that many young people at Redland Park had not sufficient outlet for their energy and their idealism, so he founded the Shaftesbury Crusade and encouraged the young people to go down to St Philips, evening by evening, and run boys' and girls' clubs, sports clubs, gymnastics classes, first aid and Bible classes and many other activities. Gymnastics seems to have been very popular, probably because it needed less space than most ball games. The Crusade flourished, larger premises were built and opened in 1900 and then extended; at one time over 4,000 people were using it weekly.

In 1897 H.W. Rudge founded and established the Dings Crusaders as a part of the Dings Boys' Club, one of the activities of the Shaftesbury Crusade. Herbert Rudge was the original driving force behind the rugby club and acted as secretary for about thirty years before becoming club president. As well as Dings Crusaders RFC, there was also another club called Dings RFC founded in 1895, and to confuse matters both teams played in the same colours – blue and white. Whilst Dings RFC played their games on a field at St Phillips Marsh called the Yearlings, just across the River Avon from Arno's Castle, Dings Crusaders played their home games on Durdham Down, some distance away. Ultimately, Dings Crusaders survived and Dings did not. It is possible that the two clubs joined forces.

The first recorded club game was played on 1 October 1898 against Elton St Michael's, which Dings lost 5-15. The next fixture was against St Mary's Old Boys, against whom matches have been played every season since then. Of the sixteen clubs that formed the original Bristol Rugby Combination in 1901, Dings Crusaders and Saracens are the only clubs to have run continually and are still playing today. In the Combination's first season (1901/02), Dings won the Cup in Division I, with Dings Crusaders 1st and 2nd XVs winning Divisions II and III. For many years, Dings Crusaders home games were played on the Downs, and at weekends residents of the High Street in Clifton (a short, narrow road leading up to the Downs, only a stones throw from the top of Blackboy Hill) made a shilling or two by helping homeless rugby teams. For years, Dings Crusaders (and their opponents) changed at a Mrs Lowe's house.

By the 1920s, Dings Crusaders were well-established within the Bristol Combination, a period when a cup competition was revived as a knock-out contest, not a system of leagues. In 1919/20, Saracens beat Bishopston in one semi-final, and Dings needed a replay to get past St Mary's in the other. In the final there was no score in normal time so extra time was played, with Dings getting the winning try. Cup rugby was very hard – too hard, many people thought, and soon the competition was scrapped.

Between the end of the war and 1948, Dings temporarily played at the Thrissell Engineering sports ground in Downend. The move to Lockleaze was brought about by Jack Steadman, who bought the ground in order that the Shaftesbury Church could branch out and establish themselves in the area. The church established a Sunday school and Boys' Brigade, but, as previously mentioned, the church never actually got off the ground as a minister could not be found to run it. In the event, the rugby club took on more and more responsibility and flourished to what it is today.

Dings Crusaders First XV, 1938/39 season. Played 28, won 27, drew 1. From left to right, back row: H. Cromwell, Tom Paul, Ernest Seward. Middle row: Jack B. Steadman (honorary secretary), N. Patten, Maurice Graham, F. Payne, K. Green, Les Fynn, William Pell, Herbert W. Rudge (president). Front row: C. Bowell, Ken McDowall, Joe Rogers (vice-captain), Arthur Payne (captain), Gilbert Tanner, Arthur Gray, Harry Brooks.

Dings Crusaders RFC Gloucestershire County Cup finalists, 1972/73. From left to right, back row: John Phillips, Gerald Williams, David Lloyd, Derek Gillingham, Robert Williams, Richard Grant, Alan Ferris, John Thorne, Tony Watkins, Martin Carter, Philip Henson, Trevor Denley, Robert Dark. Front row: Jim Austin, Paul Lloyd, Richard Hook, Philip Knowles, John Sheppard, Patrick Clark.

Dings Crusaders First XV, late 1960s. From left to right, back row: -?-, John Shepherd, Martin Carter, Jim Austin, Tom Paul, Richard Potts, Richard Hook, Roy Phibben, Graham Troote, Les Fynn (chairman), Philip Knowles, Joe Rogers. Front row: Roger Bowden, Patrick Clark, Peter Edmunds, Colin Kimmins, Ray Bowden, Gerald Williams.

Dings Crusaders Vikings, 1985/86 season. From left to right, back row: Brian Bush, Patrick Clark, John Whittaker, Jeffrey Darby, John Knight, Robert Beynon, John Phillips. Front row: David Skuse, Stan Thatcher, Christopher Butcher, Geoffrey Mason, David Lloyd, Colin Lewis, Mike Sanigar, Ramia Peraza. The Fifth XV was commonly made up of veteran players and adopted the name Dings Vikings.

Dings Crusaders celebrate winning a Keynsham rugby sevens competition in 1968. From left to right, back row: Graham Backes, Patrick Clark, Tom Paul, Richard Grant, Jim Austin, Les Fynn (chairman). Front row: Philip Henson, Roy Phibben, Graham Troote.

Dings Crusaders, *c.* 1974. From left to right, back row: David Appleton, Patrick Hennessy, Richard Grant, Jeffrey Darby, Richard Hook, Paul 'Jake' Lloyd, Fred Swift, Stephen Butcher, Patrick Clark. Front row: Chris Turner, Alan Ferris, Robert Williams, Gerald Williams, Philip Henson, Jason Henson, John Thorne.

Lockleaze Rangers, photographed in 1960, were founded by Bill Tidball of Thornycroft Close. Their first season was inauspicious, losing all of the matches played, but the league awarded the club a fair play trophy for their sportsmanship despite a number of heavy defeats. From left to right, back row: Malcolm Gray, Michael Farrant, Bill Tidball, Hedley Rylatt, Alan Stone, Roy Bull. Front row: Brian Calder, Christopher Tidball, Peter Woodland, Kelvin Grainger (club captain), David Tidball, Kenneth Purnell.

Lockleaze Community Association FC in their first season in the Church of England League 1963/64. The team started the season in grand style by beating Cadbury Heath 4-3 in a friendly match, with goals by Pat Clark (2), Eddie Coles, and Tony Blake. From left to right, back row: David Salter, Tony Fugill, Tony Blake, Melvyn Parker, Eddie Coles, Derek Berry. Front row: Colin Pitt (mascot), Clive Blake, David Jordan, David 'Wally' Woolford, Patrick Clark, Paul Irving.

Lockleaze Community Association football team 1964/65 season, pictured on 'the plateau' playing fields, Purdown. The team wore red shirts and white shorts. From left to right, back row: Fred Blake (manager), Tony Fugill, David Salter, Rodney Shorland, Paul Grivelle, Michael Berry, Patrick Clark, Tony Blake. Front row: David 'Wally' Woolford, Roy Pitt, John Pursey, Ted Norton. The club was coached by Bristol Rovers stalwart, Doug Hillard, in the 1960s.

Lockleaze CA Second XI football team, 1962. From left to right, back row: Ken Berry, Maurice Freestone, George Pegler, Billy Williams, Keith Jones, Michael Berry, Leslie Waltho, -?-. Front row: Raymond Budding, Kenneth Paul, Glen Smart, Brian Henson, Michael Lyons. The club, founded in 1962, was managed by Ken Berry, a local councillor who ran the dance hall and social club in the Gainsborough Square community building, and were successful in the Church of England Saturday league over a number of seasons.

Lockleaze Community Association FC, 1968/69 season. From left to right, back row: Derek Berry, David Scott, David 'Wally' Woolford, Melvyn Parker, John Pursey, Gilbert Cox, Tommy Morris (manager). Front row: Michael Brine, Bill Blake, Patrick Clark, Dennis Sanigar, Glyn Grainger.

The two teams representing Lockleaze Community Association Football Club, who played each other in the final of the Pirates' six-a-side soccer tournament won by the team in stripes on Frenchay Common, c. 1967. From left to right, back row: Peter Sheppard, Alec McBride, Clive Godfrey, Patrick Clark, David Morris, Tim ?. Front row: Glyn Grainger, Roger Grimmerson, Billy Blake, David Turner, John Pursey, Maurice Watts.

St James' five-a-side football team, photographed in Lockleaze School playing field, July 1967. From left to right, back row: Peter Woodland, Philip Hedges, David Connelly, Stephen 'Sammy' Stride. Front row: Kelvin Grainger, Albert Mountain, Kenny Purnell. This team were unbeaten for two years and played in the national five-a-side youth club tournament at the Crystal Palace sports arena, London. Albert Mountain, the football team manager, is the father of Valerie, the female singer in the church's production of *A Man Dies*.

One of St James' football teams played in black-and-white-striped shirts. This group of youngsters are pictured in 1964 at Lockleaze playing fields, Purdown. By 1967 the club was running four football teams. From left to right, back row: -?-, Alan Stone, Revd Brian Phillips, -?-, -?-, Andrew Connelly, Stephen 'Sammy' Stride, David Ash (?), Ronald Lloyd (manager). Front row: Stephen Bailey, Keith Balson, Philip Hedges, Stephen Bennett, Bryan Balson, Stephen 'Tiddler' Lloyd.

St James' were winners of the Gloucestershire Football Association junior cup in the 1972/73 season, beating Hanham Forest 2-1 after extra-time in the final played at Ashton Gate. Inside-right Roy Gallop scored both goals. From left to right, back row: Geoffrey Endicott, Robert Clark, John Vardy, Keith Farr, Jeffrey Darby, Roger Jarrett, Jimmy Warburton. Front row: Ian Findlay, Peter Smith, Philip Hedges (captain), Les Gallop, Roy Gallop. St James' won the Under-18 Division of the Bristol Church of England League in their first competitive season in 1964/65, and then became champions of the sixth division District League in the following season. They progressed to the First Division as runners-up in the 1970/71 season. The Revd Brian Phillips was secretary of the club, with the Revd Ernest Marvin as an enthusiastic president. Ronald Lloyd, a former inside-left with Lockleaze Rovers, was the general manager, assisted by Doug Hughes and Ken Chandler.

Shaftesbury Crusade Under-18 football team, 1972/73 season. From left to right, back row: Tony Routledge, Brian Lacey, Martin Peacock, Martin Painter, Martin English, Andrew Kirby, Anthony White. Front row: Robert Ford, Colin Clark, Robert Norman, Keith Sanigar, David Peters.

5

ORGANISATIONS

Revd Ernest C. Marvin, minister of St James' Presbyterian Church, presides over afternoon tea for members of the church's Fellowship of Youth, a group for those youngsters committed to the church and the church's teaching. It related to the national organisation of the same name and usually contained the Revd Marvin's confirmation candidates. The venue for the occasion is the flat behind the church, sometime in the 1950s.

Members of the 40th (Lockleaze Presbyterian) Cub Scouts pack outside of St James' Church in Romney Avenue, *c.* 1954. From left to right: David Weetch, David Isaac, -?-, George Pegler, Robert Weetch, -?-.

A group of Lockleaze Brownie Guides, attached to St Mary's Church, gathered in the mid-1950s. During this period meetings were held on Thursday evenings, commencing at 6.30 p.m., at St Francis' Church, Dovercourt Road. Patricia Malpas is the girl standing in the front row of the group on the left. The Brownies were organized in 1914 and were originally called Rosebuds. The girls didn't like that name, so in 1915 Lord Baden-Powell himself called them Brownies, from the story 'The Brownies' by Juliana Horatia Ewing, written in 1870.

Members of the 40th Bristol (Lockleaze Presbyterian) Scout Group assembled sometime between 1952 and 1955, the period when Revd Whitehorn was group Scout master. The Revd Michael Whitehorn, minister of St James' Church, is stood fourth from the left in the back row. The Cubs and Scouts in the group would have been sons of the first Lockleaze inhabitants.

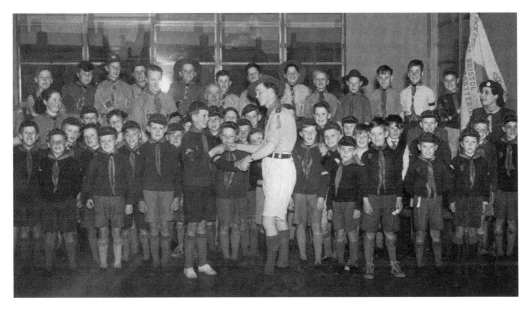

The first leaders of the group were Revd Michael Whitehorn (group Scout master), K. Farmer (Scout master), J. Thomas (Cub master), and assistant Cub mistresses Miss M. Radford and Miss J. Bell, who also acted as secretary to the group council. Other early leaders of the 40th included Mr Quartley, Mrs B. Farmer, Miss S. Woodington and Miss M. Burleton. A Scout troop was also started at Lockleaze Secondary School in 1956.

Above: A group of boys belonging to the 40th Bristol (Lockleaze Presbyterian) Scout Group in the grounds adjacent to St James' Church, Romney Avenue, *c.* 1960. From left to right, back row: Ronald Hurley, David Cox, Ivan Rudge, Anthony Bushell, K. Farmer (Scout master). Third row: Alan Mays, Jeffrey Clash, Robert Williams, Second row: Robert Hawker, George Pegler, Roger Tanner, Tony Neate. Front row: Philip Barrett, N. Smith, Martin Cox. The hut in the distance was known as 'Toc-H', later used as the community hall.

Left: Before a hut for the uniformed organizations was built behind St James' Church in 1956, the Boy Scouts, Wolf Cubs, Brownies and Girl Guides held their meetings in Romney Avenue School. This group of Scouts are pictured in the grounds of St James' Church. From left to right, back row: -?-, David Cox, -?-, Ivan Rudge, Ronald Hurley, K. Farmer (Scout master). Middle row: -?-, -?-, Robert Williams, George Pegler. Front row: -?-, -?-, -?-.

The front cover of a 50th (Shaftesbury Crusade) Company membership card for 1955-1956. Issued annually to all boys in the company, they contained details of the officers, squad members, programme, battalion fixtures, boys' obligations and uniform. That year the weekly company subscription was 3*d* for boys at school and 6*d* for boys at work.

The Boys' Brigade was founded in Glasgow on 4 October 1883 by William Alexander Smith, a twenty-nine-year-old business man, part-time soldier and loyal churchman. He conceived it to combine drill and fun activities with Christian values. When designing the Brigade's motto and crest, William Smith referred directly to Hebrews 6:19 in the King James version of the Bible, 'Which hope we have as an anchor of the soul, both sure and stedfast...' From this verse came the BB motto, 'Sure and Stedfast', retaining the old spelling of the latter word. The crest was originally a plain anchor, bearing the BB motto with a capital 'B' on either side. Upon the merger between the Boys' Brigade and the Boys' Life Brigade in 1926, the red Greek cross was placed behind the anchor to form the current emblem. The cross originally formed part of the emblem of the Boys' Life Brigade.

50th (Shaftesbury Crusade) Life Boys, 1953-54, with leaders Mr John Budd and Miss Patricia Clarke. The group of boys, aged between eight and eleven years, includes: Peter Frampton, Stephen Pople, Roger Pritchard, Patrick Clark, Terry Jarrett, Michael Watts, Michael Stevens, Douglas McGuinness and Brian Winter. The original hall floor was prone to dampness, so every time it was used for gymnastics, Stan Stokes would spread newspaper over the floor to absorb the moisture.

The 50th (Shaftesbury Crusade) Company Boys' Brigade assembled in Lockleaze School gymnasium in 1957. From left to right, back row: Terry Jenkins, Gordon Fudge, Brian Towning, Michael Dawes, Keith Smith, Brian Townsend, Terry Nicks, Clive Bull, Clive Shinfield. Third row: Roger Pritchard, Stephen Sweet, -?-, Roland Eyres, Michael Wall, Alan Davis, Terry Jarrett, Michael Stevens, John Neale, Michael Beveridge. Second row: David Woolford, Robert Munden, Brian Winter, Anthony Cox, Lieutenant Ken Sweet, Captain Joe Stokes, Lieutenant Stan Stokes, Patrick Clark, Glyn Davies, Paul Hodder, Raymond Dawes. Front row: Peter Gibbs, Ronald Lias, John Stone, David Mitchell, Anthony Jones, John Watson, Alan Elvins, Douglas McGuinness.

Life Boys and Boys' Brigade gather inside the Shaftesbury Crusade hall for the occasion of an enrolment service, 1955. Boys' Brigade activities were held mostly between September and April, with an enrolment service held in September to welcome new members to the company. From left to right, back row: -?-, Michael Morris, Ronald Cockram, -?-, Clive Bull, Terry Jenkins, Gordon Fudge, Brian Towning. Fifth row: Alan Jones, Alan Herbert, Michael Munden, Keith Smith, -?-, Terry Nicks, Paul Smale, Michael Dawes, -?-, Michael Scadding -?-. Fourth row: -?-, Michael Stevens, Alan Davis, Robert Munden, John Neale, Terry Jarrett, -?-, -?-, -?-. Third row: -?-, -?-, John Whittaker, -?-, -?-, Roger Pritchard, Maurice Watts, -?-, Michael Hodder, -?-, -?-, -?-. Second row: -?-, -?-, James Brierley, Miss Patricia Clarke, Lieutenant Stan Stokes, Pastor Albert Godsell, Captain Joe Stokes, Mr Dance, Stephen Pople, Roland Eyres, Stephen Smith. Front row: -?-, Peter Frampton, Glyndwr Davies, Brian Henson, Keith Jarrett, Timothy Williams.

Opposite below: The 50th Bristol Team of Life Boys or Junior Reserve of the Boys' Brigade, 1954. Bill Brooks, the caretaker and groundsman, a resident of Crome Road, is stood at the back. From left to right, back row: -?-, -?-, -?-, -?-, -?-, Keith Smith, -?-, Brian Townsend, Gordon Fudge, Alan Herbert, -?-, -?-. Third row: -?-, John Neale, -?-, Miss Patricia Clarke (leader of Life Boys), Mrs Edna Godsell, Pastor Albert Godsell, Captain John Budd, -?-, -?-, -?-, -?-. Second row: -?-, -?-, John Pavey, -?-, -?-, -?-, -?-, -?-, -?-, -?-, -?-, Terry Jarrett, -?-. Front row: -?-, -?-, Patrick Clark, -?-, Douglas McGuinness, Brian Winter, -?-, Roland Eyres, Timothy Murray, -?-, -?-. Lockleaze Secondary School, in its final stages of construction, is in the distance.

Captain J.A. 'Joe' Stokes at an annual Bristol Battalion camp at Weymouth. Together with his brother, he took over the running of the 50th (Shaftesbury Crusade) Company Boys' Brigade in 1952. A housemaster and teacher at Hartcliffe School, under his leadership the company were most successful, winning many trophies at battalion and district level. He left the area in 1973 to become deputy headmaster of Beacon Secondary School, Crowborough, Sussex. His brother, Lieutenant Stan Stokes, also a long-standing member of the 50th, met his future wife, Ann Seward – a helper with the Life Boys – at the Shaftesbury Crusade in Landseer Avenue, marrying in 1959. Ann later became the company pianist.

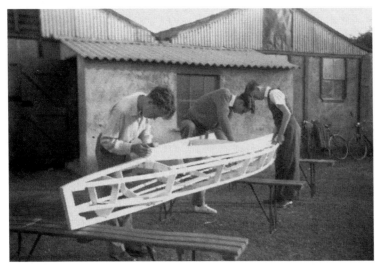

Stan Stokes organised this canoe-building activity, obtaining the plans and wood, with the boys helping to construct it. Michael Scadding, Terry Jenkins and Michael Hendy are working on the craft outside the Shaftesbury Crusade hall in Landseer Avenue. The finished canoe was taken to Winscombe camp in the summer.

Members of the 50th Company Boys' Brigade arriving at Temple Meads Railway Station in 1955, en route to Weymouth for their annual summer camp held in fields near Preston, about four miles from the seaside resort. From left to right: Michael Dawes, Stephen Smith, John Neale, -?-, -?-, Alan Davis, Michael Stevens.

Bible classes were held on Sunday mornings at 11.00 a.m. in the main hall at Shaftesbury Crusade. This one, around 1969, is being conducted by Captain Joe Stokes, assisted by Andrew Kirby. All the work of the company, especially the Bible class, was directed towards leading boys into the fellowship of the Church. From left to right, back row: Bernard Frampton, Stan Stokes, -?-. Third row: Martin Painter (half-obscured). Second row: Martin English, Martin Peacock, Keith Sanigar, Michael Beacham, -?-, -?-. Front row: Philip Stone, Terry Stone, Stephen English, Tony Routledge, Stephen Payne, Martin Pring. Albert Endicott is playing the piano.

The 50th Life Boys football team, 1953/54. From left to right, back row: Stephen Pople, Michael Watts, Richard Hook, Dennis Sanigar, Stephen Smith, Roland Eyres, Roger Pritchard. Front row: Peter Frampton, Patrick Clark, Douglas McGuinness, Brian Henson, -?-. Standing behind the team are Mr Bill Pritchard and Miss Patricia Clarke, leader of the Life Boys. Bill Pritchard was a prominent member of the Boys' Brigade and a coach for Bristol Central Swimming Club. When at camp he was responsible for the swimming activities.

The 50th (Shaftesbury Crusade) Company Boys' Brigade football team, 1957/58 season, in Lockleaze School gymnasium. There was a close association between the local Boys' Brigade Company and the school. From left to right, back row: Brian Towning, Brian Townsend, Michael Wall, Michael Dawes, Clive Shinfield. Front row: Keith Smith, Michael Stevens, Terry Jenkins (captain), Terry Nicks, Clive Bull.

The 50th Company Boys' Brigade football team in the late 1950s. From left to right, back row: Richard Newton, Raymond Dawe, Michael Stevens, John Neale, Brian Townsend. Front row: Maurice Watts, John Watson, Clive Bull, Patrick Clark, David 'Wally' Woolford, Alan 'Elmer' Davis.

The 50th Company were champions of the Bristol Battalion Boys' Brigade football league in the 1960/61 season. The trophy is the A.J. Bradley Shield. From left to right, back row: John Watts, Keith Jarrett, Richard Hook, Timothy Williams, Martin Hewitt, Paul Wootten. Front row: Stephen 'Spud' Bull, Christopher Morgan, Dennis Sanigar, David Morris, Peter Frampton.

The 50th Company PT (Physical Training) team, 1956. From left to right, back row: John Stone, David Mitchell, Peter Gibbs. Front row: Roger Pritchard, Robert Munden, Patrick Clark, John Watson, David Woolford, Roland Eyres. The partition behind allowed the Shaftesbury Crusade hall to be divided in two sections.

The 50th Company were winners of the Tudor Cup, the senior cup competition for Bristol Boys' Brigade football teams, c. 1967. The final was played at the Bristol and West Sports Ground, on the Portway. From left to right, back row: David Conlin, Paul Sweet, Robert Hatton, Michael Hayter, Geoffrey Endicott, Brian Williams, John Smith. Front row: Michael Milton, David Thomas, David Watts, Brian Leach, Ian Corrick.

The Lord Mayor of Bristol, Alderman L.K. Stevenson, inspects members of the 50th Company in Landseer Avenue on the occasion of the opening of the refurbished Shaftesbury Crusade hall, Saturday 16 June 1962. From left to right: -?-, Dennis Sanigar, Christopher Morgan, Brian Winter, Bernard Frampton, David Ford, Leslie Sanigar, David Wildblood, Maurice Cove, Geoffrey Endicott, -?-, Alan Bryant, David Lloyd. Captain Joe Stokes accompanies the Lord Mayor, with Jack Steadman behind. The history of Redland Park United Reform Church records the event:

As the work expanded the one hut proved totally inadequate, a hall and extra rooms were imperative. So in 1961 an appeal went out for funds, and throughout the next two years Redland Park church members found many ways of raising money. It concluded in a big gift day, when the Revd Norman Voice, Warden of Shaftesbury, received gifts at Redland. On 16 June 1962, a day of bright sunshine, a crowd converged at Lockleaze Shaftesbury to take part in the opening of the new buildings by the Lord Mayor and Lady Mayoress. They were shown a spacious hall, a well-equipped new kitchen and other rooms. The original hut and plunge bath had been completely re-decorated and once more the opening was followed by rugger and soccer matches.

Terry Jarrett, Douglas McGuinness and John Watson, members of the 50th Company, proudly display the Queen's Badge, worn uppermost on the left arm, awarded to them in 1960. The badge was awarded after a member completed many other awards and it could take three or more years to qualify for the Queen's Badge. It is the equivalent of the Silver Duke of Edinburgh Award, although in some ways more difficult to achieve as it covers many subjects.

Captain Joe Stokes, followed by Lance-Corporal Brian Winter, leads the 50th Company in the annual Bristol Battalion founder's day parade around the roundabout in Queen Square, Bristol, Sunday 1 May 1962. It was customary for the company who had won the drill parade competition the previous year to lead the parade. The 50th won the district drill competition shield in 1961. From left to right, column nearest the camera: Richard Neate, Dennis Sanigar, Peter Frampton, Derek Elsbury, Leslie Sanigar, Alan Bryant, Paul Sweet, Anthony Parsons, Geoffrey Strachan, Gerald Critchley, Philip Davis, Gerald Neilson, Stephen Bull, Robert Banks, Lieutenant Stan Stokes, Lieutenant John Smith. Middle column: David Mitchell, Christopher Morgan, Timothy Williams, John Watts, Stephen Bailey, Barry Watts, Brian Ford, -?-, -?-, David Ford, Bernard Frampton, Christopher Spence, Robert Williams. Far column: Patrick Clark, Stephen Pople, Philip Parrott, Michael Sanigar, David Morris, Michael Watson, -?-, Geoffrey Endicott, John Morris, David Lloyd, Raymond Whittle, Christopher Mitchell, Martin Hewitt, Captain Albert Endicott.

Brownies from St James' pack pictured in the church grounds with Purdown in the distance, c. 1953. From left to right, back row: -?-, -?-, -?-, -?-, -?-, -?-. Third row: -?-, -?-, -?-, -?-, -?-, -?-, Jeanne Carter, Diane Shattock, -?-, -?-. Second row: -?-, Linda Hill, -?-. Front row: -?-, -?-, -?-, -?-, Hilary Bennett, -?-, Jeannette Bush.

6

LOCKLEAZE SECONDARY SCHOOL

Lockleaze School first year football team, 1955/56 season. From left to right, back row: Norman Bryant, Philip Goater, Philip Andrews, Robert Munden, David Richardson, John Spence, Michael Jackson. Front row: Mr Terry Allen (PE teacher), Anthony Cox, Patrick Clark, Desmond Tippins, Philip Lanceley, Leonard James, Paul Brookman. Mr David Porter, a mathematics teacher, is stood behind the team.

Members of Lockleaze teaching staff, 1958. From left to right, back row: Mr Reginald J. Batterbury (art – head of department), Mr Robert F. Kinghorn (science – head of department), Mr David W. Porter (mathematics), Mr Eric S. Brown (music – head of department), Mr Adrian Robertson (German), Mr Kenneth A. Williams, (educational guidance – head of department), Mr Robert W. Barnes (technical studies – head of department). Middle row: Mrs M.C. Hammond (PE), Mr George L. Wilson (English – head of department), Mr Howell Thomas (history), Mr Colin B. Evans (maths – head of department), Mr New, Mr R.A. Nicholas (French – head of department), Mr John P. Rosling (physics), -?-, Rene Phipps (?) Front row: Patricia Brown (history), Mrs Daisy I. Butterworth (educational guidance), -?-, Mr Kenneth A. Edwards (deputy headmaster), Dr William N. Littlejohns (headmaster), Mrs Glenna R. Paynter (humanities – head of department), Mrs Jean E. Grasby (domestic science – head of department), -?-, Miss Paula Hubner (art).

A model of an aircraft carrier is the centre of attention for these boys during a Royal Navy recruitment visit to the school at a careers exhibition, c. 1960. Left to right: Keith Willis, Christopher Perry, -?-, -?-, -?-, -?-, -?-, Roger Evans, Paul Gardner, Timothy Wood, David Weedon.

From left to right, back row: Barry Roberts, Donald Sloggett, Tony Sleeman, Nicholas Sloper, Dennis Attwood, Michael Britten, Clive Walters, Gordon Brown, Peter Bush. Third row: Vera Thomas, Linda Davidge, Angela Baker, Margaret Lloyd, Mary Horley, Pauline Bunce, Lesley Avery, Stella Willcocks, Annette Cheesewright, Janet Green. Second row: Christine Grose, Anita Sims, Sylvia Edwards, Pearl Edwards, Mr John P. Rosling (senior physics master), Celia Slowley, Delia Walter, Valerie Ball, Jacqueline Jefferies. Front row: David Badman, Leon Bees, Richard Fletcher, Donald Bumpstead, Stuart Armsby, Quentin Nicholls, Christopher Haggett, Robin Haggett. The majority of these pupils commenced at Lockleaze in September 1956.

Lockleaze School first year cricket XI, 1956. From left to right, back row: Paul Brookman, Philip Goater, Philip (?) Read, David Radford, Jeffrey Slowley, Jeffrey Russell. Front row: Mr Terry Allen (PE teacher), Patrick Clark, Desmond Tippins, Philip Lanceley, Leonard James, David Woolford, Jeffrey Williams.

Tutor group 7L in their first year at senior school, 1993. From left to right, back row: David Rawlings, Jason Amos, Daniel McKervey, Dean Cottrell, Robert Stone, Clay Woodward, Ian Jervis. Middle row: Ben Knight, Michael Clack, Beth Millar, Lisa Davies, Veena Jhumat, Sarah Dimambro, Winston Arnold, Jamie Moore. Front row: Sasha Harris, Hayley Champion, Lindsey Egan, Heather Franklin, Mrs Gaynor La Porte, Nicola Peacock, Jennifer Gilbert, Kelsay Hancock, Leanne Clack.

Tutor group 11L, taken in May 1998, their last day at school. From left to right, back row: Ben Knight, Dean Cottrell, Ian Jervis, Daniel McKervey, Dean Scott, Jason Amos, Robert Stone. Middle row: Clay Woodward, Mr Clean Muranda (head of year), Veena Jhumat, Heather Franklin, Beth Millar, Sarah Dimambro, Jamie Moore, David Rawlings. Front row: Nicola Peacock, Leanne Clack, Hayley Champion, Mrs Gaynor La Porte, Lindsay Egan, Lisa Davis, Jennifer Gilbert. Both photographs on this page were used to illustrate a school prospectus.

Mr Eric Brown, music teacher, organised a school holiday to the Italian Adriatic resort of Rimini in 1963. In a letter sent home to pupils prior to the trip, he had this advice for 'big girls':

The Italian male has a way of looking at any reasonably attractive female as if she was the first woman he had ever seen in his life. His eyes take on an expression of stunned wonder, zigzagging from her head to her toes as he makes a mental relief map of the rolling crests and hidden valleys of this new and unexplored continent. These boys are all incredibly handsome. Don't fall for their deceptive charm. It is delusion that can end in a state paralleled only by *delirium tremens* [DTs]. Hence no Italian girl of good family is ever seen in public after 8.30. I shall control you very rigidly in this and take drastic action if any of you fall in love these Romeos.

The boys also received a warning: 'Don't try copying the Italian youths or you will wake walking down the aisle with a girl on your arm and her father close behind.

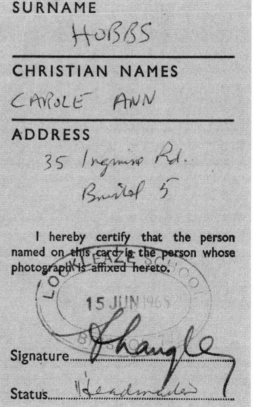

SURNAME

HOBBS

CHRISTIAN NAMES

CAROLE ANN

ADDRESS

35 Ingmire Rd.
Bristol 5

I hereby certify that the person named on this card is the person whose photograph is affixed hereto.

15 JUN 1965

Date of Issue:

Collective Passport No.

SIGNATURE OF HOLDER

Carole A Hobbs,

Signature.....

Status..... Headmaster

The identity card issued to Carole Hobbs by the Foreign Office for her visit to Spain in July 1965. The card also has the school stamp and is signed by the then headmaster, Mr Fred Langley. All pupils on the school trip to Lloret del Mar in Catalonia carried individual identity cards whilst travelling under a collective passport.

Beaufort House sports team, 1960. From left to right, back row: Mr David W. Porter (mathematics teacher and head of lower school), Barbara Critchley, Gethin Joyner, -?-, Paul Brookman, -?-, Duncan Campbell, Philip Lanceley, Keith May, Mr Duncan C. Gordon (German teacher). Middle row: Janet Shorland, Carol Dowling, -?-, -?-, David Lloyd, Trevor Denley, ? Hedges, Albert Bundy (?), Geoffrey Lewis, -?-, Richard Hutton, Mrs Maureen Barnett (French teacher). Front row: -?-, -?-, -?-.

Beaufort eight tutor group, 1970-71. From left to right, back row: Michael Thomas, Trevor Mead, Robert Davies, -?-, Glen Marshall, Marcus Sanyasi, Neil Greatorex, Mohammed Razaq, Philip Pickford. Middle row: Shirley Evans, Sheila Batten, Annette Gasson, Gillian Thomas, Elizabeth ?, Elizabeth Cox, -?-, Sonia Dixon, Diane Stone. Front row: Catherine Jones, Tony Spokes, Melford Gardner, Carvie Currie, Shafiq ?.

Form 3B photographed in the school assembly hall, 17 April 1958. From left to right, back row: -?-, Brian Dimond, Terry Lewis, John Hill, Raymond Edmonds, Alan Phelps, -?-, Anthony Pople, Roger Pritchard. Third row: Ann Waltho, Pearl Fillingham, Linda Hill, Beryl Rogers, Wendy Harding, Carole Pegler, Heather Hartnell, June Gillard, -?-, Anthony Jones. Second row: Valerie Doling, Maureen Haskins, Celia Brown, Christine Gadsby, Mrs M.C. Hammond (PE), Mr Eric S. Brown (music), Hilary Gibson, Janet Newman, Maureen Archer. Front row: Norman Bryant, Trevor Pullen, Richard Newton, John Watson, -?-, Brian Winter, Maurice Watts.

Five female members of Form 5R photographed in their classroom, 1961. Left to right: Margaret Lloyd, Celia Slowley, Pauline Bunce, Delia Walter, Angela Baker. All five commenced at Lockleaze Secondary School in September 1956.

The last pupils, Years 9 and 11, and remaining staff of Lockleaze Secondary School, 2004. Opened in September 1954, the school closed at the end of the summer term, July 2004. From left to right, back row: Adam Constantim Anil Saroe, Jamie Owen, Jake Whiteside, Sam Stephenson, Michael Chorlton, Abdi Shide, Kane McKervey, Craig Crisp, Mukthar Hassan, Hamza Ibrahim, Mohammed Adidd, Thomas Harris, James Greenough, David Jones, Michael Wise, Michael Ballinger, Jonathan Leigh, Nathan Kelly, Adam Chaplin, Jason Heath, Gareth Evendon, Andre Curry, Myeesh Brown. Sixth row: Craig Dymock, Miles Prosser, Scott Hughes, Luke Broderick, Matthew Hatherall, Mathew Milsom, Aaron Dorrington, Carl Gubb, Michael Curtis, Glynn Davies, Bradley Starkie, Jack Connolly, Stephen Moore, Robert Scott, Lee Jones, Stephen Quigg, Jonathan Connolly, Aaron Grove, Kevin Parker, Brendan Thomas, Gary Risdale, Russell Taylor, Paul Hughes, Michael Rossiter, Jamie Pepper, Jake Hacker. Fifth row: Aaron Seyton?, -?-, -?-, Andrew O'Meara, James Browning, Lee Worlock, Melissa James, Stacey Dymock, Samantha Cook, Natalie Thomas-Gayle, Louise Beaugie, Lora Smith, Christina Williams, Laura Puncheon, Katie Hobbs, Natalie Harris, Becki Bryant, Gemma Smart, Kayleigh Palmer, Sherelle Coles, Maddy Wall, Jordan Stone, Christian Bailey, Darren Clark, Kurt Hooper.

Fourth row: Candy Redman, Saffron Levenoir, Alex Hines, Rakiba Jauffur, Gemma Croome, Anna Havizavi, Sarah Benneworth, Mercedes Bennett, Terrianne Rutter, Amy Rich, Stavroulla Ioannou, Katy Woodland, Amy Hynam, Danika Miles, Laney Thornell, Keira Parker, Samantha Bailey, Katie Elvin, Louise Bond, Laura Vile, -?-, Hannacj Blanchard, Samantha Smith, Samantha Roe, Justine Nutt. Third row: Liam Ward, Richard Harmer, Anthony Hopkins?, Kevin Heath, Jordan Campbell, Neil Bond, Kerry Ryan, Shannon O'Reilly, Sarah Stoneman, Nicole Smith, Samantha Kirwan, Emma Bennett, Leanne Horsey, Suzanne Haynes, Terri Bakerville, Jodie Wood, Emma ?, Jamie White, Danny Reid, -?-, Charlie O'Reilly, Lee Clark. Second row: -?-, Barbara Gosden, Jean Beer, Mona Liss-Carless, -?-, PC Nigel Ashcroft, Maria Perrett, Philip Harper, Karen Rossiter, Neil Jenkins, Terri Skeete, -?-. Front row: Angela Golding, Sue Clark, Janet Pearce, Andy Dobbs, David Mager, Ian Miller, Chris Mercer, Jenny Browne (bursar), Philip Carter, Beverley Verwoert, Robert Smith (chair of governors), Raymond Lockey (headteacher), Martin Harris (vice-chairman of governors), Tim Cowell, Cherry Plenty (school secretary), Robin Grimes, Chris Meechan, Paul Roberts, Derek Young, Mark Wilson, Lesley Hill, Sylvia ?, Sandra Reed.

The staff team pose during the staff vs school football match half-time break, 1960. From left to right, back row: Howell Thomas, Duncan Gordon, Kenneth Williams, Leonard Davies, David Porter, Ivor Evenden, John Trenchard, Conway Artus. Front row: John Adams, Colin Evans, Terry Allen, R.A. Nicholas.

First year pupils, 1960. From left to right, back row: Stephen Bennett, Alan or Jeffrey Taylor, David Wildblood, Andrew Hedges, Melvin West, Terence Rodway, Paul Spencer, Dennis Owen, Paul Harvey. Middle row: -?-, Alan Andow, Linda Nethercote, Caroline Stiff, Jacqueline Taylor, Patricia Jones, Linda Bevan, Peter Yeo, Brian Peters, Mr Roger Stenner (chemistry teacher). Front row: Elizabeth Woodhouse, Sheila Pitson, Patricia Cox, -?-, -?-, Margaret Fry, -?-, Linda Williams, -?-, June Long (?).

Lockleaze School girls five-a-side football team, *c.* 1982. From left to right, back row: Susan Harvey, Alison Roberts, Julie Thatcher, Nicola Cole, Sarah Wood, Nicola Fudge, Joanne Jenkins. Front row: Amanda ?, Tracey ?, Claire Osborne, Rachel Hill, Hayley Mead, Marie Kelly, Donna ?. Rachel Hill, in the front row holding the ball, attended the school between 1979 and 1984.

The school play in 1962, produced by Mrs E.E. Pryce, was an ambitious production of *Antigone* by Jean Anouilh. Performed in the school hall on the 18 and 19 December 1962, this picture is of a dress rehearsal. From left to right, rear of stage: Paul Morrell (Messenger), Carole Hobbs (Nurse), Linda Davidge (Eurydice), Pearl Edwards (Antigone), Sidney Smith (Page). Front of stage: Angela Baker (Chorus), Derek Gore (Third Guard), Trevor Denley (First Guard – Jonas), Michael Dauncey (Second Guard – a corporal), Barry Roberts (Creon), Mary Horley (Ismene).

Studious expressions are evident on the faces of these pupils as they carry out experiments during a lesson in the chemistry laboratory, *c.* 1960. From left to right: Peter Bush, Bernard Gillard (?), John Grinter, Dennis Attwood, -?-, -?-.

Another picture of the same chemistry lesson, under the tutelage of Mr Kinghorn, head of sciences. Ernest Takle, the pupil with glasses at the front, is talking to Roger Brown. Robert Beynon is stood to the left of Mr Kinghorn, with David Cox behind him and Gordon 'Josh' Brown, with glasses, in the top right. Angela Baker is half-obscured.

Members of staff, 1991. From left to right, back row: Mike Haynes, John Knowler, Dave Griffiths, John Dacey, Neil Bartle, Clean Muranda. Third row: Tim Warren, Ian Dye, Chris Meechan, Andy Dobbs, Richard Dark, Ian Miller, Graham Jerrold, Philip Carter. Third row: Paul Roberts, Bob Wathen, John Burr, Peter Radford, David Archer, Mark Wilson, Tim Cowell, David Healey, Jack Murray, Graham Lees. Second row: Ann Price, Kaye Grayston, Susan Green, Rosemary White (née Watts), Susan Clark, Bridget Turner, Cathy ?, M. Speight, Mona Liss-Carless, Angela Golding, Barbara Gosden, Jaclyn (?) Skuse. Front row: Barbara Paganetto, Alison Parsons, Susan Mustoe, -?-, James Fagg, Raymond Lockey (headteacher), John Angle, Gaynor La Porte, Valerie Bradbeer, Ann Parker, Patricia Thompson (resources technician).

Members of the Lower and Upper Sixth forms on a visit to Swansea University in July 1961 in a photograph taken by Mr Colin B. Evans, head of mathematics and school bursar. From left to right: Philip Lanceley, Jeffrey Slowley, Roger Fenn, Joyce Plummer, Anthony Pitson, Duncan Campbell, Jeffrey Russell, Richard Hutton (obscured).

Form 4M, 1961, photographed in front of the music room. From left to right, back row: Mr O.W. Oldham, ? Alford, Alan Gardner, John Lane, Christopher Dickson, Martin Shorland, Anthony Hodges, Alan Taynton. Front row: Wendy Gammon, Patricia Farmiloe, Wendy Gibson, Wendy Griffiths, Lilian Siddle, June Wilton, Barbara Bakehouse, Maureen Wollacott, Joan Williams, Evelyn Allen, Rosemary Williams.

Head of music, Mr Eric Brown, conducts the school orchestra during a practice session in the main assembly hall. Duncan Campbell, principal first violin, and David Stevens are two of the violinists, whilst Roger Fenn, adjacent to the double bass, plays the clarinet. Immediately behind him, playing brass instruments, are Philip Barrett (French horn), Barry Conlin and Richard Hutton. Michael Jackson is seated in the back row playing trumpet.

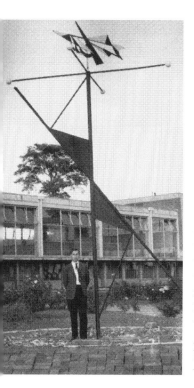

Robert Barnes, who taught at Lockleaze from 1956 until 1967 – between 1956 and 1962 as the engineering master, and from 1962 to 1967 as head of the technical studies department – beside the giant sundial and weathervane which stood outside the main entrance to the school. The main structure, 25ft high and weighing about ⅓ of a ton, was designed by Barnes and Reg Batterbury, head of art (who painted it). It was erected when the school opened in 1954, with the weather vane added in 1960. This picture was taken in 1960, shortly after the weather vane was put in position by Bob Barnes using a three-piece ladder borrowed from the building contractors who were extending the main school building at the time. When asked by the second master Ken 'Jim' Edwards if he was insured, Mr Barnes replied that he would do the job whilst the head was out as he thought he may stop him. The weather vane main body was hauled into place by the building contractor's crane in exchange for them being allowed to use the school workshops during a particularly wet weekend. A similar arrangement led to Barnes acquiring the massive steel tubes for its construction, which were arc welded together during the school holidays whilst the pupils were out of sight. The contractors refused to climb the rig because of union rules, hence Mr Barnes' exploits. At one point there were plans to remove the sundial but it was left because of the strong objections from pupils; the sundial and weather vane are still in place in 2010, despite the school's closure.

Cooks, in white, and dinner ladies photographed at the rear of the school kitchen, 1967. From left to right, standing: Audrey Sandell, Irene Critchley, Bessie Toomer, Edna Lewis, Kathleen Blake, Lily Long, Edith Williams, Trixie Williams, Irene Nicks, Florence Sparks, Rose Hodder, -?-. Seated: Evelyn White, of Landseer Avenue, kept a diary containing the menus that she prepared for the pupils and staff.

The summer of 1961 and Form 3R, with English teacher Mr Conway Artus, assemble outside the music room for their class photograph. From left to right, back row: Gerald Broadbear, Philip Parrott, David Goddard, -?-, Colin Priddle, John Turner, Douglas Mills, Geoffrey Lewis, Peter Davis. Middle row: David 'Inky' Stevens, Hans McAuley, Brenda Hanks, Sally Donachie, Susan Godfrey, Mary Robbins, Susan Brooks, Elizabeth Hill, Dorothy 'Dot' Bye, Anne Caple, Hilary French, Linda Conibear, Mr Artus. Front row: Carole Hobbs, Patricia Lloyd, Mary Shaddick, Ann Wintle, Sally Head, Valerie Ellett, Janet Neale, Gloria Radford. Most pupils in this photograph commenced at the secondary school in September 1958.

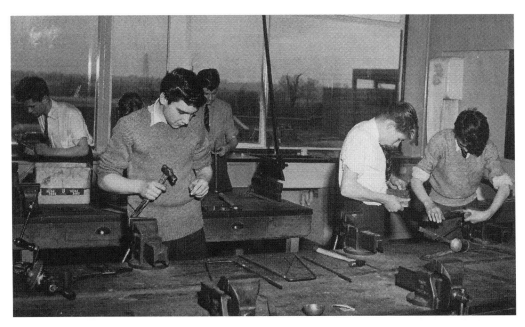

An assortment of tools and a variety of activities can be seen taking place in this metalwork class, c. 1959. Raymond Bailey is holding the ball-pein hammer with David White to his left. Both boys started at Lockleaze in September 1957. Construction work can be seen through the classroom window.

The school production of the operetta for children *The Midnight Thief*, music by Richard Rodney Bennett and libretto by Ian Serraillier. The musical was performed in school year 1967-68 on a temporary stage erected in front of the serving hatches in the main assembly hall. The story takes place in Mexico and is about a farmer with three sons who are tasked with discovering who has been stealing their father's corn. The cast were clothed in ponchos and sombreros, not to mention the glittering plumage of the bird of paradise and the helpful toad's colourful outfit. From left to right, back row: Michael Miles (Augusto), ? Partridge (?), -?-, Glen Marshall, Kevin Merritt, Terry Sherman. Front row: Julie Alford, Elizabeth Jay, -?-, Regan Toomer, Maxine Hodges, -?-, Martina Moore (Toad), -?- (Bird of Paradise).

Probably class 1G2, assembled near Tower Bridge with the River Thames behind, summer 1958. From left to right, back row: Gloria Budding, Edward Spear, Constance Winslett, Susan Winter, Alan Hampton Douglas Mills, -?-. Second row: -?-, Daphne Jones, Mrs E. Pryce (drama teacher), -?-, -?-. First row: Ann Smith, Carol Holland, Georgina Forse, Alan Brown, Carole Hobbs, Anne Caple?, Bonita Hall, Ann Bryant, Valerie Ellett. Front row: Lynne Aldus, Dennis Rowles, Wendy Skidmore, Carol Coles, Penny Barrett, Mary Robbins.

Form 4T, 1961. From left to right, back row: David Dimond, -?-, George Pegler, -?-, Edward Norton, Dennis Sanigar, Maurice Powell, Robert Williams, Philip Morris (?). Middle row: Peter Dainton, Michael Heavens, Patricia Smythe, -?-, -?-, -?-, -?-, Martin Cox, Christopher Overton, Mr John P. Rosling (physics). Front row: Valerie Pound, -?-, -?-, -?-, Adrienne Webb, Jennifer Fackrell, Ann Lyons, Janet Neale (?), Diane Breach.

Stood outside the Natural History Museum during a school visit to London with Mrs Clouse, June 1981. The trip was open to all first year pupils with the group travelling to the capital in Wessex Coaches; the Victoria and Albert Museum being another venue visited. From left to right, back row: Chantelle Haynes, Marie Kelly, Rachel Mountstevens. Front row: Julie Gregory, Donna (?). In the background, Michelle Kennedy.

A Lockleaze School class, April 1958. From left to right, back row: David Radford, Hedley Rylatt, John Spence, Keith Smith, Roland Eyres, Raymond Dawe, Jeffrey Williams, James Corbin, Richard Daly. Third row: Jeannette Whittle, Gillian Mills, Patricia Williams, Ann Hawker, Gillian Stone, Carol Mapstone, Maureen Haskings, Patricia Collings, Lindra Shore. Second row: Maureen Dixon, Margaret Perham, Maureen Worgan, Doreen Hale, Mr Adrian Robertson (German teacher), Carol Cardinelli, Maureen Cozens, Ann Walker, Janet Conibear, Diane Smale. Front row: Stephen Sweet, Roger Hurford, David Mitchell, Patrick Clark, John Stone, Paul Irving. Most pupils started in September 1955.

A number of the group who visited Weymouth in the summer of 1962 on a school-leavers' day-trip to the seaside resort. From left to right: Gloria Morales, Gillian Gomm, Lynda Jay, Mrs E.J. Mathieson (head of needlecraft), Christine ?, Pauline Cox. Their last day at Lockleaze School was 27 July 1962.

First-year pupils getting to grips with the intricacies of threading a Singer sewing machine during a needlework class. The first article made by girls in needlework lessons was a pinafore – a practical item as it was required when attending cookery classes.

As part of the preparation for finding employment on leaving school, this group of girls are being shown around a local footwear factory. The school's careers advice included visits to local employers as well careers exhibitions in the school's main assembly hall. Della Sims, who left the school in July 1961, is second from the right.

7

ROMNEY AVENUE
SCHOOLS

Romney Avenue Junior School teaching staff, 1952. From left to right, back row: Mr Tanner, Mr Davies, -?-, -?-, Mr Hague, Mr Mountain. Front row: Mrs D.E. Fahy, Mrs E. Haxworth, -?-, Mr Hammacott (headmaster), Miss Vear, -?-, -?-. The junior school opened on Monday 7 February 1949, admitting ninety-nine pupils on the first day.

Romney Avenue Primary (Infants) School was officially opened on Friday 13 April 1951 by the then Minister of Education, the Rt Hon. George Tomlinson, MP. The infants' school for 320 pupils, together with the junior school for 480 pupils, first occupied in 1949, completed the primary group on the nine-and-a-half-acre site. The cost of the school was £68,208. This view shows the dining room, on the left, and main assembly hall. To achieve architectural harmony on the site, materials similar to those of the junior school were introduced in the later building, in that aluminium units formed the classroom wings, and the facing bricks and stonework of the assembly hall, dining room, and kitchen and administrative rooms matched those used in the junior school.

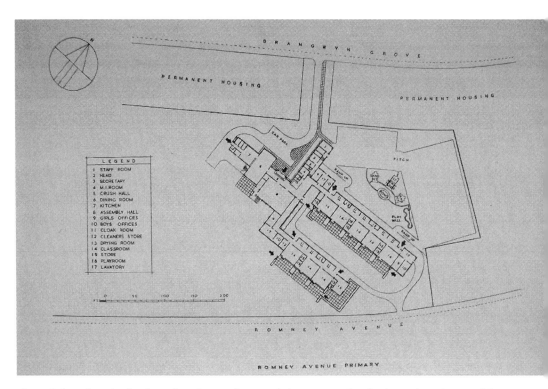

LEGEND
1 STAFF ROOM
2 HEAD
3 SECRETARY
4 M.I.ROOM
5 CRUSH HALL
6 DINING ROOM
7 KITCHEN
8 ASSEMBLY HALL
9 GIRLS OFFICES
10 BOYS OFFICES
11 CLOAK ROOM
12 CLEANERS STORE
13 DRYING ROOM
14 CLASSROOM
15 STORE
16 PLAYROOM
17 LAVATORY

Plan of the infants' school sited to the north-east of the junior school. The rather elongated layout of the school was influenced largely by considerations of aspect, contours and the narrow width of the site, and was based upon two parallel blocks of seven and five classrooms running along the contours.

Romney Avenue Juniors, c. 1957. From left to right, back row: Mrs E. Haxworth, Derek O'Keeefe, Anthony Gibbs, Brian Dimond, John Prowle, Paul Brookman, Timothy Arnold, Terry Bakehouse, Anthony Watts, John English, Robert Hedges, Christopher Butcher, Alan Emery. Second row: Paul Lewis, Raymond Short, Carole Pegler, Diane Williams, Lindra Shore, Carol Brain, Diane Shattock, Patricia Williams, Ann Hawker, Hilary Gibson, Philip Randell, Leonard James. First row: Valerie Bray, Denise Dando, Rosemary Lamb, Gillian Stone, Jane Wintle, Christine Gadsby, Anita Harris, -?-, -?-, Maureen Haskins, Pearl Fillingham, Angela Slater. Front row: Ivan Jones, Terry Salter, Trevor Pullen, Keith Smith, Alan Elvins, Rodney Smith, William Bowley.

Romney Avenue Juniors chess team, 1976. From left to right, back row: Michael Osborne, Mr David Greenland, Andrew Jones, Paul Didcott, Wayne Thomas, Mr Geoffrey Geen. Front row: Gordon Perrett, Shawn Hopkins, Robert Harmer, Kevin Hammond, Kevin Colton.

Romney Avenue Juniors Class 4, 1956-57. From left to right, back row: Mrs D.E. Fahy, Brian Flinders, Dennis Rowles, Kenneth Stevens, John Turner, Derek Bolson, Alan Hampton, Geoffrey Lewis, Robert Thompson, Aubrey Newport, Philip Parrott, Mrs Williams. Third row: Hilary French, Margaret Heavens, Jennifer Skuse, Sylvia Cooper, Patricia Lloyd, Joanna Caple, Mary Wilkins, Dorothy Bye, Jean Uzzell, Lorraine Ackerman, Linda Hewitt, Linda Conibear. Second row: Susan Winter, Ann Wintle, Jennifer Jones, Linda Meredith, Susan Godfrey, Gillian Martin, Carol Holland, Patricia ?, Patricia Dezell, Pamela Phillips, Bonita Hall, Patricia Morris, Pamela Bateman. Front row: Daphne Jones, Geraldine Whitton, Anne Bryant, Mary Shepherd, Susan Burgess, Mary Robbins, Sally Donachie, Margaret Clarke, Elizabeth Hill.

Children of Romney Avenue Infants School on an educational visit to Salthouse Farm, Severn Beach, in May 1961. The farmer, Mr J.T. Miller, is the man wearing the trilby. Robert Richardson is stood on the left at the back between two teachers. Mrs Crocker, another teacher, is stood on the far right.

Romney Avenue Juniors class, 1961-62. From left to right: Michael Batt, David Conlin, Hazel Jarrett, David Clark, Christine Treasure, Susan Cockram. This group of children commenced at Lockleaze Senior School in September 1962.

Romney Avenue Juniors Class 1, 1969-70. From left to right, back row: Tony Cook, Phillip Ellis, Steven Church, David Tippins, Malcolm Smith, David Wheeler, Jeremy Barker, Clive Budding, Colin Kenyon. Fourth row: Dean Leonard, Robert Bryant, Christopher Garrett, Mark Palmer, Stephen Perham, Terry Bryant, Colin Pitt, Gary Britton, Martin Croome. Third row: Deborah Clark, Miriam Calder, Rita Searle, Angela Payne, Christine Stephens, Beverley Partridge, Christine Bryant, Alison Adams, Alison Coombes. Second row: Christine Woodland, Karen Gray, Anne McBride, Mr George Constance, Anne Haynes, Helen Jenkins, Sharon Davis. Front row: Martin Mills, Colin Peters, Jeffrey Wiltshire, Barry Painter, Barry Hynam, Stephen Farrant.

Romney Avenue Juniors first aid group, complete with stretcher, *c.* 1952. From left to right, back row: Richard Isles, Billy Williams, -?-, Roger Donachie, Stephen Parrott. Front row: Peter Gibbs, -?-, Russell Williamson, -?-, Nigel Bly.

Romney Avenue Juniors, *c.* 1955. From left to right, back row: Martin Cox, Philip Barrett, Jack Tye, Robert Hawker, Anthony Robinson, David Isaac, -?-, Neville ?, Stephen Hall, Roger Walters, Richard Marks, Michael Lewis. Middle row: Christopher Wride, Martin Hewitt, Jeffrey Clash, Veronica Keefe, Sandra Pritchard, -?-, Angela Hodge, Rachel Adams, Christopher Overton, Robert Williams, Barry Conlin. Front row: Diane Tucker, -?-, -?-, Gillian Gomm, Rita ?, Janet Conibear, Lilian Siddle, Lynda Charlton, -?-, Lynda Jay, Joy Swindlehurst, Barbara Hale.

Romney Avenue Juniors photographed outside of the school's main entrance, *c.* 1957. From left to right, back row: -?-, Brian Chaney, Maurice Freestone, Stephen Stride, Peter Laver, Malcolm Gray, John Knapp, Terence Upton. Middle row: Michael Berry, Leslie Waltho, Robert Hall, Stephen White, -?-, -?-, Albert Bundy, Stephen Bull, Steven Purnell. Front row: Gloria Manning, Patricia Trigg, Pauline ?, Rowena Cardinelli, Valerie ?, -?-, -?-, -?-, Gillian Worgan, Marilyn Gray, Linda Ward. The majority of these pupils were born in 1947.

A group of pupils photographed in the classroom during their final year at junior school, 1961-62. From left to right, front desk: Helen Mitchell, Lynda Thorpe, Robert Lott, Bernice Hawker, Sylvia Wadman. Seated behind: Anne Pike, Paul Moore (?), Gillian Skuse, Michael Batt, David Clark, Christine Treasure, Susan Cockram. Possibly Elizabeth Wintle in the foreground.

Romney Avenue Juniors, 1961-62. From left to right, back row: Philip Curtis, -?-, Neil Horton, Anthony Humphries, Tony Marshall, Richard Grinter, Alan Cramp, Timothy Pike, Leslie Henson. Third row: Pauline Wheeler, Veronica Shoreland, -?-, Christine Pring, Valerie Nash, Alexandria Winslett, Jean England, Sarah Beach, Janice Long. Second row: Hilary Hendy, Jane Pavey, -?-, -?-, -?-, Mrs Rosemary Dodd, Susan Davis Margaret Hook, Rosemary Hobbs, Carol Radnedge, -?-. Front row: Ian Sloggett, Paul Corbin, Steven Jeremiah, Alan Dibbins, Colin Dibbins, Geoffrey Dunn, Philip Smith.

Romney Avenue Juniors fourth year netball team, 1962. From left to right, back row: Hazel Jarrett, Bonita Gammon, Helen Kralshaw. Middle row: Mary Wollacott, Margaret Jeremiah, Joy Head, Alison Jones, Susan Cockram, -?-. Front row: Margaret Stevens, Judith Strachan, -?-, Andrea Davis, Margaret Corbin.

A large crowd of family members and siblings watch the junior school sports day races in the summer of 1956. The competitors in this running race have adopted fancy dress and carry umbrellas for the event. The houses behind the spectators are homes on the south-eastern side of Brangwyn Grove.

Romney Avenue Juniors, 1978-79. From left to right, back row: Wayne Pegler, Justine Heales, Paul Worgan, Paul Newland, David Stutt, Susan Allen, David Nichols. Second row: Mr Colston Meese (headmaster), Karen Coupland, Paul Haynes, Jane Knight, Nicola Fudge, Nicola Belcher, Matthew Stevens, Gary Knight, Mr 'Rolly' Walters. First row: Susan Jeremiah, Helen Adey, Mandy Gleeson, Elisa Knight, Julie Fearon, Jennifer Abrahams, Rachel Cox. Front row: Nicholas Slade, Andrew Carling, Martin Amos, Paul Leaworthy, John Cromarty.

Romney Avenue Juniors, 1961-62. From left to right, back row: Jeffrey Newman, Christopher Bushell, David Conlin, Brian Williams, Robert Lott, Dean Sims, Vivian Hudd, Robert Hitchings, Roger Hurley, Davi... Clark. Second row: Gillian Skuse, Julia Thomas, Doreen Bakehouse, Joy Head, Christine Treasure, Lind... Thorpe, Susan Vickerman, Alison Jones, Bernice Hawker, Susan Cockram. First row: Elizabeth Wintl... Bonita Gammon, Anne Pike, Sylvia Wadman, Mrs Fahy, Hazel Jarrett, Lynne Naden, Gillian Cottle, Hele... Mitchell. Front row: Michael Batt, Philip Sleeman, Mervyn Lewis, Andrew Malpas, Craig Horton, Pau... Moore, David Adlam, Paul Searle.

Romney Avenue Juniors football team, 1976/77 season. From left to right, back row: Paul Didcott (goalkeeper), Mr Walters. Middle row: Michael Jefferies, Nicholas Spokes, Gary Moss, Gary ?, Alan Jefferies. Front row: Samuel Payne, Martin Hook, Kevin Hammond (captain), Jerry ?, Terry Gregory. The team was a combination of third and fourth year boys.

Romney Avenue Juniors Second XV rugby team, 1955/1956 season, taken outside of the school's main entrance. From left to right, back row: Raymond Whittle, Philip Barrett, Robert Hawker, Paul Gardner, D. Wilmott, Roger Walters. Middle row: David White, Lawrence Long, Anthony Bushell, Jeffrey Clash, Raymond Bailey, Roger Tanner, -?-, Mr Tanner. Front row: Alan Searle, -?-, Michael Lewis, Brian Henson, Martin Cox.

Romney Avenue Juniors, c. 1955. From left to right, back row: Mr Norman, Martin Nightingale, Jeffery Sloggett, Paul Gardner, -?-, -?-, Keith Willis. Middle row: Brian Henson, Raymond Bailey, ? Bushell, Timothy Wood, -?-, Anthony Godfrey, Philip Jennings, Paul Hodder. Front row: Christopher Perry, -?-, ? Irwin, -?-, Pauline Smith, Peter Morris, Leigh Coomber.

Romney Avenue Juniors nature club, 1957. From left to right, back row: Wendy ?, Sandra Winter, Margaret Heavens, Bonita Hall, Linda Meredith. Middle row: Patricia Malpas, Joanna Caple, ? Williams, Patricia Lloyd, Dorothy Bye, Jean Uzzell, Elizabeth Hill, Sally Donachie, Mr Gregory. Front row: Pamela Phillips, Carol ?, Philip Parrott, Kenneth Stevens, Linda Hewitt, -?-, ? Hedges, Philip Hedges. Dorothy Bye is holding a glass display case containing a stuffed owl; the other two display cases hold dead butterflies and moths.

This photograph, which appeared on the front page of the *Bristol Evening Post* in 1976, is of Romney Avenue School pupils standing outside Bath Guildhall Market with Bath Abbey in the background. From left to right: Ailsa Rook, Alison Lewis, Christine Nye, Sarah Smith, Tania Woods and Susan Gregory, who plays a treble recorder. The rest of the group play the ubiquitous school descant recorder.

Romney Avenue Juniors Class 3, 1964-65. From left to right, back row: Christopher Knapp, Andrew Williams, Colin Hewitt, Robert Richardson, Tommy Harper, Andrew Price, Richard Gurney, Brian Wadman, Martin Painter, Christopher McGrane, David Peters, André Kirby. Third row: Sandra Williams, Julie Naish, Elizabeth Paul, Stephanie Pitson, Linda Jones, Wendy Annette, Hilary Kirby, Josephine Conlin, Ruth Nelmes, Valerie Cooper, Patricia Morris. Second row: Shirley Davis, Jacqueline Deas, Catherine Jones, Elizabeth Jay, Mrs Joan Silverthorne, Carol McKenzie, Elizabeth Taylor, Rachel Dodd, Diane Stone. Front row: Martin English, David Pike, Barry Ryley, Kevin Owen, Ronald Tarrent, Mark Leonard, Roger Partridge, John Osborne, Stephen Barker.

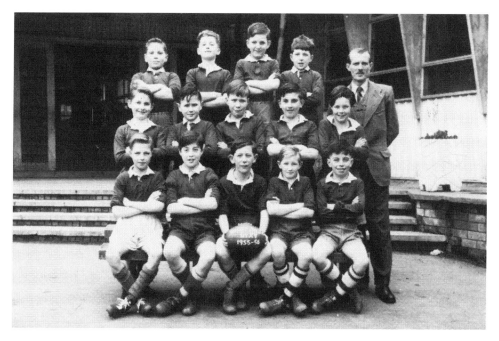

Romney Avenue Juniors First XV rugby team, 1955/56. From left to right, back row: -?-, -?-, -?-, George Pegler. Middle row: John Knight, -?-, -?-, David Cox, Martin Hewitt, Mr Davies (RE teacher). Front row: -?-, -?-, Robert Beynon, Philip Hedges, -?-.

Romney Avenue Juniors football team, 1969/70. From left to right, back row: Christopher Garrett, David Maxwell, Geoffrey Neville, Steven Church, Mr Michael Day. Middle row: Martin Mills, Michael Tidcombe, Dean Leonard, Christopher Burrows, Colin Peters. Front row: Martin Bakehouse, Clive Budding, Colin Pitt, Steve Buckland, Martin Greenaway.

Romney Avenue Infants, 1967. From left to right, back row: Russell Smyth, Mark Smith, -?-, Christopher Batt, Andrew Hewlin, Kevin Warfield, Robert Atwell, Robert Gurney, Robert Hawkins, Stephen Curley (?), Lee Milton. Second row: Kay Feltham, Robert Peters, Gillian ?, Robert Conlin, Mark Allen, Wayne Lewis, Beverly Davies, John McBride, -?-. First row: -?-, Simone Burchill, Mark Davies, Beverly Perham, Hazel Jarrett, Miss Sheila C. Connett, Sandra Strickland, Richard Harris, Sonia Capaldi, Gary Isles. Front row: Andrew Coleman, Jacqueline Lane, Lesley Grey, Teresa Garrett, Andrew Haynes. This was former pupil Hazel Jarrett's first teaching placement after leaving Fairfield Grammar School.

Romney Avenue Juniors fourth year netball team, 1969/70 season. From left to right, back row: Mrs Susan Clark, Julie Foale, Jane Gurney, Lorraine Dowling. Front row: Sally Garrett, Kim Street, Julie Hook, Larraine Froud, Jennifer Campbell.

Romney Avenue Juniors First XV rugby team, 1958/59 season. From left to right, back row: Mr Hammacott (headmaster), David Lloyd, Brian Edmonds, Michael Truman, Stephen Bennett, David Llewellyn, Mr Tanner. Middle row: Graham Hatherall, -?-, Christopher Spence, Paul Sims, Stephen Hook, -?-. Front row: Gordon ?, Philip Henson, ? Winters, Raymond Whittle, Philip Hedges.

Romney Avenue Juniors Under-11 football team were winners of the Coronation Cup in the early 1990s, a competition for small Bristol schools, the definition based on the number of pupils. The adults stood at the back are from left to right: Mr Leslie Andrew, headteacher of Romney Avenue Juniors; Mr Robert Smith, the chair of governors of Romney Avenue Juniors and Lockleaze Secondary School; Mr Raymond Lockey, headteacher of Lockleaze Secondary School. These Year Six boys were in their last year at junior school prior to moving to secondary school.

Headteacher Mr Leslie Andrew and school secretary Mrs Christine Strode sat with a group of pupils on the children's last day at Romney Avenue Juniors, 31 July 2004. The school officially closed on 31 August, amalgamating with Romney Avenue Infants School to form Lockleaze Primary School, which opened in 2006. This is one of a series of photographs taken by Robert Smith, chair of governors, to record the closure of the school.

8

A MAN DIES

Roy Harkness, portraying Christ, celebrates the Last Supper with four of his disciples during the ABC Television production of *A Man Dies*, transmitted on Sunday 26 March 1961. From left to right: Denis Potter, who played Judas Iscariot, John Sweet (John), Roy Harkness, John Walters (Peter), Graham Lloyd (Matthew).

In 1959 the Revd Ernest Marvin, minister of St James' Presbyterian Church, Lockleaze, and Ewan Hooper, a newly-arrived actor at the Bristol Old Vic Theatre, conceived the idea of writing a modern passion play in which youngsters would participate. They would perform in their normal clothes and to a background of contemporary music; in 1960 it was rock 'n' roll.

The first production of *A Man Dies* was a 'theatre in the round' presentation in St James' church hall at Easter 1960. Technically it did not provide a complete circle for the audience, seated on three sides of the hall, leaving floor space as well as the stage for the dancers and actors. In one corner of the stage was the group of musicians, The True Tones, comprising Richard Smith (vocals), Michael Gwilliam (lead guitar), Jeff Donadel (rhythm guitar), Ron Cooper (drums) and Andy Reynolds (tea chest bass). Richard Smith and Mike Gwilliam wrote the music to the lyrics provided by Ernest Marvin and Ewan Hooper. The performance, with Kenneth Maughan playing the part of Christ, was played to a full church hall for a week.

In 1961 the play was presented in the Colston Hall, Bristol, the largest auditorium in the West Country, on three nights during Easter. The last night of that year's production was seen by representatives of ABC Television, who were sufficiently impressed to want a 45-minute adaptation on television. An extract from the play, starting with the events on Palm Sunday and ending with the resurrection, was televised by ABC Television (Birmingham) on 26 March. A second adaptation, which started with Moses and ended with the Nativity, was televised on *The Sunday Break* by ABC Television (Manchester) for Christmas 1961 under the title *Man in Time*.

The musicians involved with the televised productions were, in Birmingham, Richard Smith, Mike Gwilliam, Keith Harris, Bob Harris and Jim Callaghan, and, in Manchester, The Tuxedos, consisting of Paddy Dunn, David 'Wally' Woolford, Ken Neil and Ted Wilson, with Valerie Mountain singing the female vocals on both occasions. In 1961, a single was released of 'Gentle Christ' and 'Go It Alone' on the Columbia record label featuring Valerie Mountain and the musicians who appeared on the ABC Television (Birmingham) transmission.

A more ambitious production at the Colston Hall at Easter 1962 was once again under the general umbrella title of *A Man Dies*, but it incorporated most of the material from *Man in Time*. The venue was booked for six nights and, except for the Easter Saturday night, there were packed houses. It was decided to give the play and everybody a rest in 1963, but a new version in 1964, 2 hours 15 minutes long, was extended in scope to cover the major events of the biblical account of God's action in history, from Moses to Pentecost and the early Church. Music that was new to the production was the work of David Mallett, a seventeen-year-old Winchester College student.

The Colston Hall was booked for a four-night run, from 2-6 March, a fortnight before an engagement at the Royal Albert Hall on 24 March. Before either of these productions, EMI recorded most of the songs and music on a long playing (LP) record on Columbia 33SX.1609. Recorded at Abbey Road Studios, it featured Valerie Mountain, Ricky Forde, and The Strangers – Geoffrey Rudd (lead guitar), Richard Gummerson (rhythm guitar), Andrew Parker (bass guitar) and Mervyn Wilson (percussion). The full text of the new production was published as a paperback book.

In the Albert Hall the dance area was the whole of the arena, so for the first time it was able to incorporate everybody who wished to be in the play. The final cast included 120 seniors and eighty juniors, with Roy Harkness as Christ, John Kirby as Judas, Sylvia Cooper as Mary, Roland Williams as Joseph and Paul Wootten as Peter. ABC Television was present to film the whole of the play. For the previous fortnight they had been filming at St James' and in the youth club and they had cameras installed on the coaches from Bristol to London. The result of their endeavours was a 1 hour 40 minute feature on Easter Sunday night.

In 1966, the fifth performance in Bristol over a six-year period had a major difference from its predecessors. The previous performances had all been public ones and advertised as such, but the 1966 production was a private one; private in that those who wanted to attend had to join the St James' Theatre Club first. This came about because of the Lord Chamberlain's refusal to grant a licence for a public stage performance of the play as, 'It has been his considered policy not to licence any portrayal of Christ on the stage.' A method of circumnavigating this ruling was to form a theatre club, membership of which was essential before purchasing a ticket, although joining the club and obtaining a ticket could be done at the same time. Mark Roman and The Javelins were now providing the male vocals and music, with Valerie Mountain, who appeared in every production except the first, as the 'girl singer'. Cast members included: John Kirby as Judas, Paul Wootten as Peter, with Gloria Manning and David Connelly as Mary and Joseph. The performance on 2 March 1966, with Robert Fry as Christ, was the last time *A Man Dies* was staged by members of St James' Church and Youth Club, Lockleaze.

An early rehearsal of the play in St James' church hall, 1960. Left to right: Bernice Hiscox, Alan Davis, Kenneth Maughan, Jean Glover, Pamela Henson, Denis Potter, Eddie Fudge. Kenneth Maughan, a twenty-one-year-old apprentice, portrayed Christ in the first production. Here he is depicted carrying his 8ft-cross to Calvary. This is how a *News Chronicle* newspaper article of 11 March 1960 describes the scene:

> The girls are in short tight skirts and sweaters. The boys are in Edwardian or Italian dress or jeans and sports shirts. Leading their mad whirl is a short youth [Potter] with ample hair curling over the collar of his knee-length jacket. His contorting legs in the black drainpipes make him look like a drunken spider. He is Judas Iscariot.

Above: The Tuxedos during a rehearsal in St James' church hall, 1961. From left to right, the band members are: Ken Neil, Paddy Dunn, Ted Wilson and 'Wally' Woolford on drums. Richard Smith, the lead vocalist, is centre stage with the Revd Ernest Marvin.

Left: The teenage instrumentalists who accompanied the production of *A Man Dies* on stage at the ABC Television (Birmingham) studios, 1961. From left to right: Keith Harris (rhythm guitar), Bob Harris (bass guitar), Mike Gwilliam (lead guitar), Richard Smith (vocals). Valerie Mountain is seated behind the microphone. Out of picture is the group's drummer, Jim Callaghan. Seated at the front of the stage from left to right are cast members: Sid Welch, Christine Gadsby, Bernice Hiscox, -?-, Michael Heavens Christopher Butcher, Diane Heath.

Teenage girls portraying a Jewish crowd in Galilee dance the 'Hora' during the production of *A Man Dies*, presented by ABC Television's religious programme for teenagers *The Sunday Break* on Sunday 26 March 1961. The programme, introduced by Neville Barker, contained extracts of the play. Clockwise: Pamela Henson (white top with back to camera), Diane Heath, Bernice Hiscox, Diane Oaten, Carol Billingham, Jean Yeomans, Jean Glover, -?-, Dorothy Leach. Wendy Griffiths and John Kirby are the couple stood on the upper platform with Denis Potter and Lynda Henson on the lower level to their left.

Margery Baker, the director of ABC Television's production of *Man in Time*, gives instructions to Paulette Kirby, 1961. In an article entitled 'All in a programme's work', Margery, who directed *This is Your Life* from 1969 to 1973, describes her involvement with the youth of Lockleaze:

For us it started in Bristol, in St James's Church Youth Club at the top of one of the innumerable hills in that town. Twelve days, seven nights, four hundred bottles of coke and eight hundred cigarettes later it was transmitted from Manchester. The hall we started in is attached to the church. Here, at 8 o'clock on a Wednesday evening with the Revd Ernest Marvin, vicar of St James' – our cast was gathered. Well some of our cast. We never had all of them at any one time until transmission! "E's working late Miss', "E's in the pub, Margery', 'They're playin' billiards', "E works on the boats – it's a late shift', 'It's his night for working the coffee bar', or "Er mother bashed her – she's bad!' were just some of the excuses.

We started with what we'd got. Ernest Marvin read the script (into a microphone in order to be heard!) – a narrative starting with the Exodus and culminating in the birth of Jesus. And the form was simply that each time he stopped speaking, the boys got up slowly and painfully clutching a girl, a fag and a bottle of coke, they went through the motions of jiving; while the band – three guitars and an over-enthusiastic drummer (and all of them amplified to a crescendo of sound) beat out a rhythm to which one of the boys or Valerie Mountain sang. It took three whole evenings – dozens of temporarily shattered love affairs (or jive affairs) and all the wiles of the units and the wisdom of Ernie (we all called him Ernie by now since the kids did too – in their politer moments) to sort it out and keep everyone happy – or happy enough to turn up for rehearsals.

We pressed on. By Saturday we had some kind of pattern, though inevitably, some of the 'Ding, Dong' girls would be missing and the 'So Tired, So Weary, So Worn' girls would be lost in the desert set with the flick-knife boys. We had – or hoped to have – a full cast on Sunday since the rehearsal would be after church and the cast would be there. We still hadn't had time to rehearse a fight sequence between the two toughest boys in the club, Graham, six-feet and fifty-inch chest, and Eddie, front teeth missing since gang-fighting. So I asked them to come round to the hotel in the afternoon to do this, and they came and had tea with us.

Church was quite an experience too. Simple, modern, packed to the doors. Lots of singing, prayers in the teenage idiom and a down-to-earth chat from Ernest, followed by coffee, cakes and a bang-on rehearsal. Suddenly, we knew it was going to be worth it – it was going to click. When we left Bristol to go to Manchester the chorus was 'Cor – no rehearsal tomorrow then? When're we going to see you again?'

Saturday in Manchester Studio One. And the invasion by the coach-load. They swarmed into the studio – invaded the canteen, necked in the circle, and were 'taken bad' at frequent intervals. The crews recognised that they were outnumbered and marvellously responded to the noisy enthusiasm. Boys climbed on cameras and booms – picked up earphones and had chats with the gallery. The girls all subscribed to the theory that cameramen are wildly attractive and the competition was fierce.

So Sunday at last. We lost a coach-load of girls for an hour – our baritone lost his voice – but everyone found, suddenly the urgency of the moment and caught on and held. The red light went on – hold your breath – into the Ding-a-Dong song without a hiccup – and that's it. At any rate, that was it for us – *Man in Time*.

Weekly dances were held at St James' Youth Club in the church hall on Thursday evenings. Most of those who attended the dances became involved in the passion play. This photograph from 1961 features, from left to right: Bernice Hiscox, Pamela Henson, Allan Cole, Christine Gadsby, Sid Welch.

A version of the play, entitled *Man in Time*, which started with Moses and ended at the crib, was presented by ABC Television (Manchester) at Christmas 1961. From left to right: Geoffrey Corbett, Stuart Forbes and Michael Heavens depict Jews in the wilderness during their escape from Egypt.

Valerie Mountain sang the female lead vocals in *A Man Dies* from 1961 to 1966. Pictured in 1961 with Richard Smith, the Weston-super-Mare girl with the urchin haircut first sang in a church pantomime – her father, Albert, was an elder of St James' Church. She aspired to a performing career while in her teens, singing with dance bands and appearing in a Colston Hall show when seventeen years old. By 1960 she had joined the Cliff Adams Singers and appeared in the Big Show in Blackpool. In 1961, a single was released on the Columbia record label of 'Gentle Christ' and 'Go It Alone', featuring Valerie, which brushed the British charts. This was followed in 1962 by her version of the title track of the film *Some People*. An album produced in 1964 included twenty-six songs from *A Man Dies* featuring Valerie, together with Ricky Forde and The Strangers.

Richard Smith, with his distinctive hair, was the lead singer in the early productions and co-wrote the lyrics to the original songs. Richard, aged nineteen in 1961, a laboratory assistant with ICI, made his first guitar for £3 from a design he saw in a magazine. Later he saved up to buy one and joined a rock group.

St James' church hall, around 1961, and Michael Lyons of Flaxman Close, Lockleaze, and Terry Upton of Ludlow Road, Horfield, present fine examples of the then fashionable and distinctive Teddy boy hairstyle.

A break in rehearsals for this group of youngsters provides an opportunity to get to know one another better. Seated from left to right: Carol Alford, Lorraine Ackerman, Patricia Hart, John Kirby, Wendy Griffiths, Carol Holland, Cliff Ashton, David Morris, Christine Ashton.

In previous years, Ernest Marvin and Ewan Hooper had relied musically on a group of instrumentalists coming together specifically for the occasion. In 1964, an experienced group of musicians accustomed to working together, The Strangers, were brought in for the performance at the Royal Albert Hall and the recording of the album. The four members of the band are the centre of attention in the back seats of the coach bound for the Royal Albert Hall. From left to right: Geoffrey Rudd, Richard Gummerson, Mervyn Wilson, Andrew Parker.

One of the Wessex Coaches that transported the cast to London parked in Kensington Gore, opposite the Royal Albert Hall, with the Albert Memorial and Kensington Gardens in the background. A deposit of £150 had to be paid to put on the play at the Royal Albert Hall, with ticket prices ranging from 5s to 12s 6d. A letter was sent out to all the youth clubs and schools in the London area advertising the event.

Roy Harkness and members of the cast alight outside the Royal Albert Hall from one of the Wessex Coaches that transported the cast members from Lockleaze to London, 24 March 1964. A camera crew from ABC Television, which accompanied the cast on the coach, was present to film the whole of the play. For the previous fortnight they had been filming at St James' and in the youth club.

The final cast list at the Albert Hall included 128 seniors and eighty juniors, not to mention forty technicians and ninety adult helpers. All these had to be taken to London from Bristol in the early morning, fed and rehearsed in the afternoon in an unfamiliar building. It appears that the meal provided was not to everyone's liking! From left to right: Stephen Davis, Dorothy Blackwell, Shirley Lawrence.

Above left: Ricky Forde, a Bristol singer, was the lead vocalist in the Albert Hall production of *A Man Dies* and on the EMI album of the songs from the passion play in 1964. Behind him is Richard Gummerson, rhythm guitarist with The Strangers. Ricky Forde sang lead for The Cyclones, specialising in Roy Orbison numbers in which he excelled. He toured with Billy Fury, Joe Brown and Eden Kane and the local talent was one of the West's first singers to tour Germany in the wake of The Beatles.

Above right: Ernest Marvin attempting to direct, organise and control the teenagers in St James' church hall during one of the many rehearsals of *A Man Dies*; a scene often repeated during the seven years of the play's existence.

A group of teenagers in St James' church hall, 1964. From left to right: -?-, Robert Fry, -?-, Mary Robbins, Cynthia Carless, Loraine Trusler, Sylvia Cooper, -?-, Raymond Whittle, Terry Upton.

Members of the team who operated the lighting for the play taking a fish and chip break late one night while installing the platforms and lighting in the girders of the roof structure of St James' church hall. This roof space is no longer visible with the addition of a false ceiling. From left to right: Geoffrey Banks, Michael Thorpe, David Morris, Roger Meredith, Roger Chaney, Ronald Baker.

A break in rehearsals provides an opportunity for these four girls to buy refreshments from the 'tuck-shop' in the church hall. From left to right: Susan Tainton, Sally Jones, Marlene Winstone, Anne Waltho.

Paul 'Bruce' Wootten, John Kirby, Terry Upton and Malcolm Gray pose for the camera in 1966. All four were involved with *A Man Dies* for a number of years, from its early productions until the last performance. Paul Wootten played the part of Peter, and John Kirby portrayed Judas from 1964 to 1966.

Left: The 'modernist' era hits St James' church hall at a rehearsal of the production in 1966 with, from left to right, Peter Davies, Ann Jeans, Cynthia Carless and Loraine Trusler. Cynthia wears the then fashionable madras check shirt, which was de rigueur for female Mods. Three years after this picture was taken, Loraine married Martin Carter, a fellow Lockleaze pupil; sadly she died in 1974 at the age of twenty-six.

Below: Gloria Manning, who played the part of Mary in the 1966 production at the Colston Hall, and David Connelly, who portrayed Joseph, during a rehearsal in St James' church hall. John Grinter is second from left, and Malcolm Gray is on the right, dancing with Christine (surname unknown).

Fashions have changed considerably since the first performance of the play in 1960. Robert Fry (left) who played Christ in the 1966 production, together with Peter Evans, who portrayed Paul, talking with Ernest Marvin at rehearsals in the Colston Hall, February 1966.

Mark Roman and the Javelins were the instrumentalists for the final production of *A Man Dies* performed at the Colston Hall in March 1966. From left to right: Valerie Mountain, Ernest Marvin, Geoffrey Coles (bass guitar), John Curry (drums), Mark Roman (vocals), Stephen Rice (lead guitar).

Other titles published by The History Press

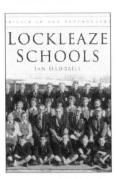

Lockleaze Schools

IAN HADDRELL

This fascinating collection of over 200 images of Lockleaze and Romney Avenue Schools have been compiled from the archives of the local schools and from former Lockleaze resident's personal collections. Featured are class photos, sports events, staff and pupils, with each image being accompanied by an informative caption. This work offers a photographic record of the schools from their post-war origins to school reunions in the 1990s.

978 0 7524 4754 4

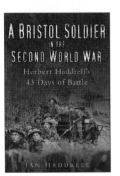

A Bristol Soldier in the Second World War:
Herbert Haddrell's 43 Days of Battle

IAN HADDRELL

Having been lucky to survive a German air raid on his Bristol home, Herbert Haddrell's personal account of the harrowing experience of being called up and sent to Normandy, where he was seriously wounded after 43 days of battle, is a fascinating and moving story. Using Herbert's recollections and some valuable letters, diaries and accounts of fellow soldiers, this book reveals the tale of a nineteen-year-old caught up in the midst of one of history's darkest moments.

978 0 7524 5169 5

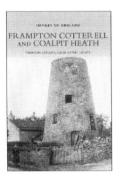

Frampton Cotterell and Coalpit Heath

FRAMPTON COTTERELL LOCAL HISTORY SOCIETY

This collection of over 200 images of Frampton Cotterell and Coalpit Heath has been compiled using photographs from the archives of the Frampton Cotterell and District Local History Society and from local resident's personal collections. This pictorial history will delight anyone who has lived in or has associations with Frampton Cotterell and Coalpit Heath, inspiring memories of more tranquil times and a more peaceful village life.

978 0 7524 4411 6

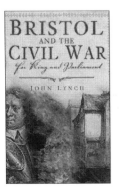

Bristol and the Civil War: For King and Parliament

JOHN LYNCH

In the seventeenth century Bristol was the second city of England. It was the main west coast port, an internationally important entrepôt and rich trading centre. The loss of Bristol in 1645 was therefore a huge blow to the Royalist cause. This book is surely one of the most important written on the Civil War in recent times. Its radical reinterpretation of the pivotal role of England's second city will ensure it a place on bookshelves of anyone interested in the most turbulent years of the seventeenth century.

978 0 7524 5214 2

Visit our website and discover thousands of other History Press books.

www.thehistorypress.co.uk